The Busy Homeschool Mom's Guide™ to
Romance
Nurturing Your Marriage
Through the Homeschool Years

Heidi St. John

Real Life
PRESS

The Busy Homeschool Mom's Guide™ to Romance:
Nurturing Your Marriage Through the Homeschool Years

Published by Real Life Press
Vancouver, Washington

©2010, By Heidi St. John

Photos by carolynsmithphotography.com ©2010 All rights reserved.
Cover design by David Sorrell | davidsorrelldesign.com

All scripture quotations, unless otherwise indicated, are taken from
the New King James Version . Copyright 1982 by Thomas Nelson, Inc.
Used by permission. All rights reserved.

Scripture taken from the HOLY BIBLE, NEW INTERNATIONAL
VERSION. NIV COPYRIGHT©1973, 1978, 1984 by Biblica, Inc, ™.
Used by permission. All rights reserved worldwide.

All rights reserved. No parts of this book may be reproduced in any form
without permission in writing from the publisher, except in the case of
brief quotations embodied in critical articles or reviews.

All inquires should be addressed to:
Heidi St. John
c/o First Class Homeschool Ministries
1400 NE 136th Ave.
Vancouver, WA 98683
email: heidi@fchm.org
www.firstclasshomeschool.org

Printed in the United States of America
ISBN 978-0-9844323-0-1

ENDORSEMENTS

Few manuscripts can make me cry; as I neared the end of it, this one did. Homeschool moms, set some time aside to read this book from cover to cover and you'll find yourself thinking back to the days of 'That Girl'.

Author/Speaker Heidi St. John is about as real as they come; I trust you will discover this as you ponder over each page. Upon completion, you'll want to answer the call to action "That Girl" will ask you to make. I know I did. Highly recommended to homeschool moms everywhere!

GENA SUAREZ, PUBLISHER,
THE OLD SCHOOLHOUSE® MAGAZINE

This book is invaluable in giving practical advice on how to keep your marriage thriving during the homeschool years. Even for those that have a good marriage, this book has the ability to take that marriage to a great marriage.

This is a book for all couples in a day when marriage is under attack and none of us are immune.

MIKE SMITH, ESQ., PRESIDENT,
HOME SCHOOL LEGAL DEFENSE ASSOCIATION

A healthy marriage is one of the foundations upon which every homeschool dream rests. We live in a world where culture, busy schedules and economic pressures all war to undermine even the best Christian marriages. Every woman will find Life between the covers of this remarkable book. Do yourself and your husband a favor. Buy it. Read it. Become the marriage partner the Lord created you to be.

JANE LAMBERT - AUTHOR,
BEFORE FIVE IN A ROW AND *FIVE IN A ROW*

Our culture tells us that the chances of having a good marriage are about the same as winning the lottery: everybody wants to win, but only a few lucky ones are ever going to get it just right. And we think, "If only. . ." (Sigh).

Heidi St. John enthusiastically presents a very different message. In this lively and transparent book, she helps us see what God had in mind when He designed men and women to actually become one flesh in marriage. It's not a lottery, it's a commitment.

With hard-earned wisdom and zany humor, Heidi lays out a very practical, relevant guideline for keeping our marriages intact, even under the highly specialized demands of homeschooling. Be encouraged! I know I was. . .

DIANA WARING, AUTHOR/SPEAKER

FOREWORD

My wife and I have traveled across America speaking at homeschool conferences since 1994. We've spoken to tens of thousands of Christian couples about the Lord's purpose in homeschooling and His passion for Christian marriage.

Sadly, in the past few years we've seen increasing numbers of single homeschool parents trying to move forward with the homeschooling dream even though their family has been decimated by divorce. Moreover, we've talked to thousands of Christian men and women who are hanging by a thread-- dangling above the abyss of divorce because of pornography, adultery, addiction, abuse or simply exhaustion.

No marriage is immune from divorce. I know elders and deacons, Bible teachers and counselors who have fallen into the pit of divorce and to be honest, most have never recovered. Nor have their children. Each of them would have sworn on a stack of Bibles that divorce could never happen in their home—but they were wrong. They thought they were immune. They weren't.

Divorce leaves a scar that causes the children of divorce to walk with an emotional limp for the rest of their lives.

The enemy wants to destroy your marriage. He wants to

destroy my marriage. He wants to undermine our spiritual lives, cut short our physical lives and he wants to hurt your children in the most painful way imaginable. And he'll gladly use our sinfulness to accomplish his agenda. But God offers hope. A window into God's heart for marriage is found in the pages of this book.

I have been deeply encouraged by Jay and Heidi St. John's heart for Christian marriages. Their hearts ache for the tens of thousands whose lives are entangled in the enemy's web of lies and deceit. And I thank God that they've done something about it.

The book in your hands is a lifeline for those who are drowning in the tsunami of divorce that is sweeping Christian homeschool marriages across America. Take hold of it as if your marriage depends on it. It very well may.

I've been working hard on my marriage now for nearly forty years and this book gave me important new insights into finishing strong. I know it will inspire you too.

Blessings,
Steve Lambert
Publisher of *Five in a Row*/Conference Speaker

DEDICATION

To my amazing husband, Jay ~

Of all the wonderful qualities I love about you, one stands out: you make me want to be more like Jesus.

Thanks for laughing (and crying) with me as I wrote about our "real" life together in the hope that others would be encouraged by our journey.

Your love has helped me find That Girl again, and your example of selfless, loving leadership inspires me every day.

It is my great joy to be your homeschooling wife.

I love you!

-h

ACKNOWLEDGEMENTS

There are a number of amazing people whose names should be appearing in lights on this page . . . without them this book would not have been written.

Grandma and Grandpa Forsberg - for hot Olvaltine with toast and every moment you invested in my life—thank you.

Savannah, Sierra, Skylar, Spencer, Summer, and Sydney, I love you so much! I am totally blessed to be your mom. Daddy and I can't wait to see all that God has for your lives unfold as you walk with Him.

Steve and Jane Lambert, for reading the initial draft of this book and believing in the message God had laid on my heart. We love you immensely and are honored to call you our friends.

Diana Waring, for speaking so honestly into my life nearly ten years ago. I praise God for your life and ministry to homeschoolers!

Makayla, Carolyn and Victoria, for giving of your time and creative talents in order to transform the vision of "That Girl" into a reality. What a team you are! Looking forward to next time!

Patty, Carie, Lou, and Jerry for all those red marks, thank you. I now understand "em dashes". Thank you for helping this fledgling writer to put her thoughts onto paper. You are a gift!

The staff, leaders and families of First Class Homeschool Ministries. It is our joy to work alongside you. Thanks for being part of the incredible work that God is doing at First Class!

Contents

Foreword..7

Introduction....................................13

1. A Cord of Three Strands 23

2. "That Girl" 37

3. White Space 55

4. Virtual Reality 67

5. Homeschool Headache 81

6. Being Naked 105

7. Parallel Lives 121

8. Moment of Truth 135

9. When It Hurts 147

10. Love for a Lifetime 161

INTRODUCTION

Why Your Marriage Matters

*"Love is not a place, to come and go as we please,
It's a house we enter in,
and then commit to never leave"*

~ "Love is not a Fight" by Warren Barfield

It's Saturday afternoon and I have just finished talking with a mom who is struggling in her marriage. As we spoke, her pain became more than she could articulate, and the tears flowed freely. She longed for an intimate relationship with her husband, but it seemed to elude her.

Like many homeschooling moms, she started out with high hopes—a picture of a perfect family that she had seen grace the cover of a homeschool magazine was imprinted on her mind. She and her husband had a plan. Now, with four kids under age ten and a baby on the way, she was beginning to realize her life was probably not going to look like the picture of the family she had memorized from the cover of that magazine. And her marriage was feeling the strain, too.

Over the past ten years, I have had many conversations like this with homeschool moms. The fact that is that homeschooling adds a whole new dimension to marriage. If we're not ready for it, the Enemy can use it to drive a wedge between a husband and wife—no matter how committed they are. I realized more than ever that marriage needs to remain the primary relationship in the family. It's never been more important than it is now, especially for homeschooling families, because your success as a homeschool mom and as a family depends on two things: Your relationship with the Lord and with your husband.

Her story is like so many other homeschooling moms I have spoken with over the past ten years.

As I wrote this book, God did an amazing work in my heart. I became reacquainted with a girl I knew a long time ago; I call her "That Girl." In the pages that follow, you will meet her. I hope she resonates with your spirit as she did mine. That Girl is inside each busy homeschool mom. She is the woman God created us to be. She is the girl we can be, by God's grace, and even though she is well aware of her flaws, she sees herself through the eyes of the One who made her.

I am also going to challenge you as the Lord challenged me: be real. When I talk about being real, I'm talking about not being embarrassed or ashamed to admit it when you have had a bad day with your homeschool, or when your marriage is struggling. Being real requires that we look deep into our hearts to find out what the source of our struggles are. Most of the time, we are not real because we are prideful. And pride is a killer.

Are you ready to be real? Because I believe that as you are real with others and honest about the everyday joys and struggles of homeschooling and marriage, you will find a freedom that is seldom found when you are hiding behind the facade of the "perfect" homeschool mom. So here we are. Lesson one: The "perfect" homeschool mom doesn't exist.

And that's okay.

Reality Check

I'm going to go out on a limb here, and kick our discussion off with a strong statement. Are you ready? Here it is: I think homeschoolers are really good at pretending. It's so easy for busy homeschooling moms to buy into the myth that they should have it all together when the reality is, that on this side of heaven no one has it all together. We like to pretend our marriages are perfect and we think it encourages others when they hear about our successes instead of our struggles. But it's not true. We encourage each other by walking out faith in the midst of trials.

True encouragement is found in staying the course and being honest about the struggles you're facing. When you're honest, it's easier to pass on what God is teaching you through that struggle to another busy homeschool mom. Other moms need to hear what you have been learning as you follow the Lord in this life. Homeschool mom, it's time to get real. And the reality is that life is difficult. As Jesus said so well in John 16:33 (NIV), "In this world, you will have trouble!"

Maybe it doesn't sound very spiritual, but for all the homeschooling books out there and the excellent resources that are available, the reality is that homeschooling makes marriage more challenging, not less. Now before you start looking up my e-mail address to send me a scathing rebuttal, let me say

> *We encourage each other by walking out faith in the midst of trials.*

I think *homeschooling is well worth the effort*—but you should not sacrifice your marriage on the altar of home education. That is not God's heart for homeschooling families. It's certainly not His heart for your marriage, either.

Everyone knows that parenting is a lot of work. Many mothers have sacrificed their marriages on the altar of good parenting. The same thing can be true of homeschooling. But when we place our children as the priority of our time and energy at the expense of our husbands, we're missing God's heart for the home. The priority is the marriage.

Firm Foundation

God says marriage is the primary relationship in home, so naturally, it's the first relationship the Enemy will try to tear down. 1 Peter 5:8 tells us, "Satan prowls around like a roaring lion, seeking someone to devour." I like to visualize this lion, prowling around outside our home. Whenever my husband and I find ourselves at odds with each other, I try to

> *The reality is that homeschooling makes marriage more challenging, not less.*

remember that lion. The imagery of scripture is a powerful tool.

Believe me, Satan knows full-well how important the marriage relationship is. A thriving marriage is absolutely key to successful homeschooling.

It's the glue that will hold you together when you think you can't take one more second of adjectives and multiplication problems. Not only that, but if you take the time to nurture your marriage above (yes, that's above) all the other relationships in your home, you will find as your children leave your home, you and your husband still have things to talk about. And you might even look forward to some alone time at the end of a busy day. Ahhhh. The end of the day. But that's another chapter.

Hope Floats

This book is about hope. And you know what? Hope floats. It really does. It bubbles to the top when everything around it is sinking. Romans 15:4 says God's word was given to us so that we might have hope. So let's look closer at His heart for your marriage, even as we hold it up to the light of reality. God's heart is that your marriage would thrive—and do you know what else? God cares about all those little things that we take for granted, including romance. God's heart for your marriage includes quiet evenings away from the kids, moonlit conversations about your hopes and dreams, and a partnership that encompasses every area of your life, including your homeschool.

I've written this book to give you encouragement and hope for your marriage. In the pages that follow, you will discover that I am just a homeschool mom like you. And like many of you, I am also a woman who has been deeply affected by divorce within my own family.

Finally, there is no formula. It's important to say that right up front. I don't have a magic formula to give you: "Five steps to a trouble-free marriage" is really just a myth, although it might sell more books. Instead of offering you a formula, I want to encourage you to love your husband as God designed you to love him. I also want to challenge you to be real about your marriage—the good, the bad, and the fragile.

> *Part of the blessing of being fragile is that it forces you to fall on your knees and talk to the One who knows exactly what you need.*

It's not bad to be fragile. Part of the blessing of being fragile is that it forces you to fall on your knees and talk to the One who knows exactly what you need. I know. I've been there.

I'm the mom who has watched the school bus go by and wondered what those "other moms" do all day. My husband has watched me have total meltdowns, and he has helped remind me that this homeschooling journey I am on is as much about me as it is about our kids. Homeschooling has changed the dynamic of our home, and has had a profound impact on our marriage. Is homeschooling hard? You know it is. Do I ever want to give up? Only every other Tuesday!

Two things keep me going on the days that I want to give up:

1. Jay and I understand why we are homeschooling.

2. We are partnering together with a shared vision for the homeschool years.

These two elements have been crucial to the success of our marriage where homeschooling is concerned. On the days when we need encouragement, we assess that partnership and vision. And then, we continually yield "our" plans to the Lord. It's part of being "one flesh."

Thank God, His mercies really are new every morning. Let's find encouragement together as we discover how loved we really are and how even a busy homeschool mom can make time to nurture her marriage. It's not as hard as you think—and it is more important than you may realize.

CHAPTER 1
A Cord of Three Strands

WHO I AM IN CHRIST

"Whom have I in Heaven but You?"
~ Psalm 73:2

*It is a foolish woman who expects her husband to be
to her that which only Jesus Christ Himself can be . . .
Such expectations put a man
under an impossible strain.*
~ Ruth Bell Graham

Allowing the Lord to Meet Our Deepest Needs

Every marriage has its defining moments. Our first "defining moment" came just about three weeks after our wedding.

I clearly remember driving over to see my mom after our first real fight (or at least it felt like a real fight at the time).

"No one ever told me that marriage would turn out to be regular life!" I said as I collapsed onto the sofa. "Somehow I signed a piece of paper that gave me a new roommate that will *never* move out!"

I'll never forget my mother's wise response. She listened to me cry, and then she quietly reminded me that it was not Jay's job to meet every need that I had.

"What?"

This was a new concept for me and at nineteen years old, I didn't really want to hear that my Prince Charming was not going to be able to meet every single need I had. Never mind that by that time, he had probably figured out that his Sleeping Beauty had some issues of her own!

After I had been there for about half an hour, she gently walked me to the front door and told me it was time to go home to my husband.

My real need was too deep for my husband to meet and I had a lot to learn about where my true significance comes from. Larry Crabb suggests that many of us stand at the wedding altar and silently repeat the vow, "I give myself to you for the rest of my life for you to meet all of my needs."

The truth is, we all have profound needs that cry out to be satisfied.

When Jesus met the woman at the well, He saw a woman in great need. She had been around men for many years apparently, given that she had been married several times and was living with another man. Yet with all her striving, she found that her deepest needs remained unmet. In John 4, we find that Jesus' loving response to her was to tell her that she was looking in the wrong place. Jesus knows that, like the woman at the well, none of us can find true or lasting peace apart from a daily surrendering, a pouring out of our spirit to Him and maintaining a living, growing relationship with the One who created us.

As the Lord becomes our source of strength, we find refreshment for our spirit. This truth is so important for us to grasp. If we are not sure of who we are in Christ, homeschooling can easily become either our identity, or a source of frustration rather than joy. Over the years, there have been many times when I have found myself up against the "homeschool wall." I have often found myself weeping on the

> *As the Lord becomes our source of strength, we find refreshment for our spirit.*

floor in my bedroom, frustrated because of my apparent inability to teach a certain child or because I wanted to give up altogether. Sometimes, I confess, I want my husband to do what God has asked me to do at home. Homeschooling is teaching me that I need to find my strength in the Lord alone.

In Psalm 27:1, David cries out, "The Lord is my strength." The only real way we can discover that strength is to spend time with God. Why? Because just like marriage is the foundational relationship in the home, our relationship with Christ is foundational to our very being. It is what sustains us.

Most moms I know desire this time with the Lord, but making the time seems difficult. It doesn't need to be.

A New Kind of Quiet (and "Quiet Time")

Do you remember having quiet time? You know, that time of your life when you got up early, brewed a cup of coffee and spent time with the Lord? I remember those days well. I looked forward to them when I was working and Jay was still at Multnomah University. Kids came into the picture after we had been married for two years, making my quiet time not so quiet. A few years later, I started homeschooling. In terms of my devotional life, it was like having a big vacuum suck up my time, my energy, and even my desire to spend time with the Lord. For a few years, I muddled by, squeezing in my quiet time where I could: sometimes, it was early in the morning with a nursing infant, and other times, it was late at night, after the house was quiet and I was sitting in bed with my husband.

However, nagging thoughts of what I was sure was the Lord's disappointment in my seeming inability to find regular time with Him kept me from growing closer to Him. I longed to be able to have "my time" back again, but the reality was that life had run me over. Literally!

My sweet husband was pouring his extra time and energy into me, trying to help me figure out why I was so discouraged. But even he came up short. It was as if he were pouring water into a bottomless well; it was never enough.

Our relationship with Christ is foundational to our very being. It is what sustains us.

With his ministry schedule and my responsibilities at home, we found ourselves struggling in areas that we never imagined we would struggle. There was a tension between us. I wanted to give up.

As with all struggles, it eventually came to a head. I knew I could not keep the walls from closing in on me without hearing from the Lord. One winter morning, I found myself up at 4:30 a.m., crying softly in the early morning light, and praying for a renewed vision for my role as a wife and homeschool mom. I had reached the end of myself. And that's exactly where I needed to be.

> *I had reached the end of myself. And that's exactly where I needed to be.*

A Watershed Moment

The Northwest holds a beauty unmatched by any place that I have ever been. God's spirit spoke to me that February morning. As I watched the sun rise over Mount St. Helens, I felt His love surround me. I have had a few watershed moments in my life and this was one of them. God spoke to me so gently that morning,

"Why are you striving? I love you. I see you.

You are infinitely precious to Me. Your worth does not depend on your ability to find 15 minutes alone with Me in the morning. If you are weary, it is because you have forgotten that I am your source of strength. I long to spend time with you, and as you do, please remember the beautiful children that I have entrusted to your care. I long for you to teach your children of My great love for them. Seek Me with all your heart with your children. Don't worry so much about trying to find time to spend with Me alone; spend time with Me in front of them. I'm not distracted from listening to you by the noise of a chattering infant. Your children playing Legos on the floor don't bother Me at all. Spend time with Me and let your children see you do it."

Hearing God's voice in the stillness of that February morning changed me forever. Not in the sense that I don't struggle with making sure I draw water from the Well that will never run dry, but in the sense that I was set free from doing it by rote. I now knew that my time with God was just as valuable to my children as it was to me; and in the setting of homeschooling, having my devotions with the kids has turned out to be the single most impacting thing about our homeschool journey.

Strength for the Weary

Are you weary? God promises that as you seek Him, you will find rest and strength for your soul. It is His heart for you. A friend of mine once said, "Heidi, if God had a refrigerator, your picture would be on it!" Why? It's because I am a daughter of the King!

Homeschool mom, so are you. As you find that your strength comes from Him, you will discover that out of the overflow of the heart, your love for your husband will grow.

When we are depending on the Lord to meet our deepest needs, Paul's words found in Philippians take on new meaning:

"And my God will meet all your needs according to his glorious riches in Christ Jesus." – Philippians 4:19

Notice the above verse says "ALL." It doesn't say "some" or "most," but it says that He will meet "all" of our needs. It doesn't say how He will meet our needs and I have found from experience the way He does it is often not what I expected. But at the end of the day, we can trust Him to do what He promises to do.

Since I am loved completely by God and can trust God completely, I should not be anxious, but rather accept His peace and rejoice in His presence. I don't need to turn to my husband to meet my every need—I can trust God to meet them. Even through what can feel like endless loads of laundry mixed in with reading, writing and math, He is able!

God's Word promises that His mercies are new every morning. Or every naptime. Or every laundry day. He's got it covered. Rest in Him. If you are in a season of your life that defies the word quiet, it's okay. God understands where you are.

> *God's Word promises that His mercies are new every morning. He's got it covered. Rest in Him.*

So What Does THAT Look Like?

After I felt the Lord give me permission to look at my quiet time with new eyes, I began to look at our family time, especially the beginning of our homeschool day differently. I usually don't tell people exactly how we homeschool, because I honestly believe that what works for our family may not work for another family.

However, I am going to share with you how we start our day. Don't consider this a mandate. Instead, think of it as something to pray over for your own family. It may be that God will use it to open your eyes to new ways that God's spirit would work in the hearts of your children at the same time He is teaching you. It's multi-tasking at its best!

We start our day off almost exactly where I left off as a very young mother: in God's Word. We don't do anything fancy—I just choose to go through God's word passage by passage.

After we read for about ten minutes, the older children and I quietly write down what God has said to us through His Word. This has always been my simple way of studying God's Word: to sit in His presence and ask Him to speak to me. God has used my surrender of what I thought was just for me (my quiet time) to show me something wonderful about the way He speaks to us through His Word. Truly, I am always amazed at how He speaks to the children through the simple reading of His Word in the same way He speaks to me!

The lessons may be simple, but often they are very profound as well.

A Little Child Shall Lead Them

There have been so many times that God has used our children to speak truth into our lives over the past eighteen years. But as we have spent time in His Word with them, those times have been more profound and life-affirming than we had ever hoped or dreamed they would be.

One time, we were reading about God's defining the twelve tribes of Israel, and how the Levites were called apart. As usual, after we read the passage, the children and I wrote in our own private journals what we had learned from reading the Scriptures that day. I don't always do this, but for some reason, I asked the kids if they would mind sharing what they wrote.

Without hesitation, our then eight-year-old son said, "Mom! *We are the Levites!* God wants us to minister to the people and He will take care of us like He took care of the them!"

Unbeknownst to our son, God had used him to speak to us. God's timing is amazing.

I was speechless. With tears in my eyes I called my husband at work.

Unbeknownst to our son, God had used him to speak to us. God's timing is amazing. This was during the week that Jay and I had decided to be obedient to God's call on our lives to minister to the homeschool community. It meant that Jay would step down from a good-paying job as a pastor and take on the faith-based life (and salary) of a missionary. We knew God was asking us to give everything to Him and God used His Word and our little boy to confirm that we were making the right decision.

Over the years, I have come to believe that as we yield our lives to the Lord, He will provide. This is as true in your marriage as it is in your homeschool.

Spend time with Him. Get into the Word. Listen for the voice of the Lord. If you want to gain insight into your marriage, carefully consider how dependent you are on

> *If you want to gain insight into your marriage, carefully consider how dependent you are on the Lord in your personal life.*

the Lord in your personal life. There is a place inside of each human being that is reserved for God alone. He made you so that only He can enter there. No one else can love you like He can and no one can be the kind of friend that He is.

He *is* the greatest love you'll ever know. Praise God! In His great mercy, He has created for us a chance to see a glimpse of the love He has for us. One of the great ways He does that is through marriage.

Allowing God to change your heart as you work on your marriage is one of the most challenging things you will ever face, but it is also one of the most rewarding. It reminds me of the words to a favorite hymn, "Tis So Sweet To Trust In Jesus;"

> 'Tis so sweet to trust in Jesus,
> Just to take Him at His word;
> Just to rest upon His promise;
> Just to know, Thus saith the Lord.
> Jesus, Jesus, how I trust Him!
> How I've proved Him o'er and o'er,
> Jesus, Jesus, Precious Jesus!
> O for grace to trust Him more."
> *Lord Jesus, this is my prayer.*
> *Help me trust you more.*

CHAPTER 2
That Girl

WHERE SHE WENT ...
AND HOW TO FIND HER AGAIN

"If a woman is beautiful before the age of forty, she had something to do with it. If she is beautiful after the age of forty, her husband had something to do with it."
~ Anonymous

Who Is "That Girl?"

Do you remember "That Girl?" You know the girl I'm talking about: her spirit is unfettered, her hopes are high, her schedule is uncluttered. That Girl is a dreamer. She still flirts with her husband. She looks in the mirror and is filled with awe at the body that God has given her. She does not see stretch marks; she sees the unmistakable signs of motherhood. She does not lament over impending physical changes in her body, because she does not know that they are coming.

Sometimes I wonder whatever happened to that spontaneous, flirtatious girl that Jay wrote love songs to. Even though Jay and I have a wonderful, strong marriage, it is still easy for me to think of myself in the light of the grocery store checkout line magazine covers. You know, those magazine covers that tell me how I should see myself. The trouble is, magazines lie. The culture that we live in has its priorities all wrong. We need new thinking if we are going to be the women God created us to be.

> *The culture that we live in has its priorities all wrong. We need new thinking if we are going to be the women God created us to be.*

A few years ago, I began to pray specifically that God would help me be the girl that Jay married. I am not saying that I was asking to be nineteen again—goodness knows I don't want to go back and re-learn some of the lessons of my twenties—but I needed to see myself with new eyes. As much as I longed to be, I knew that I was not That Girl any more. Between pastoring, pregnancies, newborns, homeschooling and home making, I had somehow lost sight of the girl that I was when we were first married. My husband noticed, too. Time and stress had created a certain distance between us. Most people wouldn't have noticed it because from the outside, we had it all together.

In our case, the distance showed up in many areas of our marriage. Jay was at work too much, and I found myself caring less and less. We stopped leaving little notes for each other on the bathroom mirror. We kept right on going as if nothing was different. You see, that "distance" I am talking about didn't happen overnight. It took me a few years of being too busy and Jay being too absorbed in his work before we started to notice.

For my husband and me, our marriage has never reached a crisis point. But like many couples, we had taken our marriage for granted. Slowly, we had become so involved with other people and with raising our kids, that we had little time left over at the end of the day for each other. We had stopped *dreaming* together. With a full-time ministry position at a growing church and young children to raise, LIFE was in full swing.

One morning, my husband's parents offered to take our children out for breakfast, so Jay and I took the rare opportunity for uninterrupted conversation and headed to our favorite coffee shop. After a few minutes of sipping lattes and enjoying pumpkin scones, I sensed that Jay had something on his mind. What he said surprised me.

"I miss you, Heidi. Are you in there somewhere?" he asked.

"You *miss* me?" I did not understand what he meant, until he began to talk about things I had not thought about in what felt like forever: date night, weekend getaways, long drives for no reason. He missed the woman that lit candles in the bedroom and who wasn't embarrassed by the sight of her own body. He too sensed the distance between us, and it was troubling him.

> *Jay missed That Girl and when I finally stopped to think about it, I missed her too!*

Please understand, Jay is my closest friend. He was not criticizing me: He really did miss me. He missed That Girl. Frankly, I knew exactly what he was talking about.

It's funny how certain conversations stand out as unforgettable. I remember that conversation in the coffee shop as clearly as I remember our first kiss and the day Jay proposed to me.

I think it's because that conversation forever changed

the way I viewed my role in our marriage. Jay didn't miss me *literally*—I was there all the time (at least physically). He missed That Girl. When I finally stopped to think about it, I missed her too!

The next few weeks provided many opportunities for me to think about the girl I was versus the girl I had become. I also had time to think about how quickly time was passing. Had we already been married for ten years? If the first ten went by fast, I could only imagine how fast the next ten would fly. As I write this book, it occurs to me that the next ten years are already gone; we recently celebrated our 20th anniversary.

The Homeschool Vortex

Somehow, I had been sucked into the homeschool vortex. Do you know what I mean? It's a place where time doesn't just stand still, you actually forget that time is going by! My days were all about the children, curriculum, and crock pots. From the moment my feet hit the floor, I was "all homeschool mom all the time." As I struggled to figure out how this homeschool thing looked (and I think I made every mistake a busy homeschool mom can make), I forgot to nurture That Girl! I now understand why the famous "denim jumper" became the required uniform for so many homeschool moms: that's what they're wearing in the vortex!

Now, I've met a few busy homeschool moms over the years who claim that there is no such vortex, but I have been inside it. Trust me, it's there. And if you think it's not there, you are setting yourself up to fall right in. In fact, you may be inside it and not even know it!

The homeschool vortex is tricky because most of the time, you're in it before you can say "Classical Education!" There is no time for romance inside the vortex because in the vortex, Latin is more important than lingerie. Legalism is the official language and laughter is lost as homeschooling becomes more and more wearisome. *Believe me, it's possible to be inside the vortex and not even know it.*

I am forever grateful that my husband threw me a line and pulled me up out of that place. At the time, I was too exhausted to appreciate what my life would have looked like if I had stayed there even

> *There is no time for romance inside the vortex because in the vortex, Latin is more important than lingerie.*

one more minute, but I am sure that I would never have found That Girl without the patient, loving pursuit of my husband.

Romance Redefined

In the months that followed, I did some soul searching. I realized that if I wanted to be That Girl again, I needed to recognize that my husband—not our homeschool—needed to be my priority. It was time to revisit our romance.

The longer I've been married, the more my idea of romance has changed. When we were dating, my idea of romance was an "I love you, baby!" phone call before a test or an impromptu meeting under the streetlights that lit up our college campus. My beloved would leave love notes for me and I would find them in the funniest places: in my car, inside of textbooks, under my plate in the cafeteria. He went all out and I loved it!

Twenty years and six kids later, my idea of romance has changed. Jay's has too. My husband is as attractive to me with dish soap on his hands or a grinning little girl on his lap as he was when he sang the lead in his rock-n-roll band, Saint John, probably even more so because we now have years of shared experiences that serve to strengthen our romance.

I don't know about you, but when my husband sees a need and goes out of his way to meet it, I can barely contain my love for him! His love, lived out in practical ways, is romantic. Why? Because true romance is love lived out. And real life includes dirty dishes and piles of laundry.

When I stop and think about it, the reality is that it was not the notes, the flowers, the moonlight, or the poetry that I really loved; *it was the thrill of the being pursued.* That was the way we lived out our love: Before dishes and diapers, there was date night.

Now, as a busy homeschool mom, the thrill of the pursuit includes ordinary things. Here's the tricky part: the homeschool vortex is a no-romance zone. If you want to be That Girl again, you've got to start back at the beginning. You've got to start romancing your husband.

Yes, the homeschool years may redefine how that romance is lived out, and yes, it will require more effort on your part. But trust me, busy homeschool mom, the blessing you will receive as you pursue your husband will be worth it!

Don't Scare the Mama

Every home has its quirky little rules. In our house, quirky rule #246 is: *Don't scare the mama.* For some reason, I am one of those individuals who does not recover gracefully from a child jumping out at me in the dark. I can think of a thousand scenarios over the past twenty years that have ended up under the "Don't scare the mama" clause in our marriage. For the sake and sanity of the mama, any practical jokes involving plastic spiders, pretend injuries, or other potentially scary scenarios get left at the door.

That rule really is all about me. In the interest of allowing me to live to see my grandchildren get married, I've asked my kids to help me keep my adrenaline at what might be considered normal levels. Sometimes they forget and I wind up the unwitting victim of a practical joke, but for the most part, we have come to an agreement.

My point is that there are some things you need to do just for you. Take care of yourself. Busy homeschool moms who are burned out, stressed out, and tired are not very romantic. If you want to find That Girl again, you might need to take a look at some things about you that need to be addressed.

Only you can determine how much rest you need and how much stress you can take. Only you can decide how many activities you can take on before other people around you start to suffer the consequences of an "over-done" busy homeschool mom. If you feel better about yourself as a person, and more confident in the way you look and feel, That Girl will be easier to track down.

Everything I Needed to Know About Romance I Learned in Third Grade

It started in grade school. I will always remember recess at the little private school that I attended in Portland, Oregon. Like all school children, we had a recess routine. If it wasn't raining, we played our favorite recess game, "boys chase the girls." The rules were pretty simple: the girls ran around screaming, the boys captured them and carried them back to the big wooden fort in the middle of the playground. Several boys stood watch over the fort to make sure some sneaky little third-grader didn't get in and release the captives.

Even at such a young age, the thrill of the chase was on our minds. We loved it. Once the girls were captured, they made "soup" out of water mixed with mud and basically called for help until the recess bell rang. It was third-grade bliss.

This grade school game went on for at least two years, but one incident still stands out to me: At some point, the boys quit. Yep, that's right. They quit. The girls were horrified. The boys sent a representative to inform us that they had decided they were *tired* of chasing the girls. They wanted the girls to chase them for a change.

We did, but it wasn't as much fun for either the boys or the girls. After a day or two, the boys decided they would rather chase the girls, but that occasionally, they would like for us to chase them. I didn't know it then, of course, but this is exactly how God made us to be.

At the end of the day, romance is about pursuit. I like to use the word *pursue* as a verb when I think of romancing my husband. When I pursue him or when he pursues me, it is love in action. That pursuit says, "I love you!"

Most women yearn to be pursued by their husbands. I believe that this is because God has created us uniquely to be responders. Yet pursuing my husband felt foreign to me, which brings me back to those instinctive feelings I noticed as a grade schooler. The only difference

> *If you feel better about yourself as a person, and more confident in the way you look and feel, That Girl will be easier to track down.*

between then and now is that I had forgotten that determined look that flashed across little Johnny's eyes when the boys had decided that they finally had enough! One-sided relationships are wearisome. When I put my grown-up self back in the playground for just a moment, it made perfect sense. Why wouldn't I pursue my husband?

In fact, when I stopped to think of what that would actually look like in practice, I felt like a little wire in my brain short-circuited. What did that look like, anyway?

If I was going to be That Girl, I needed to find what made my husband tick. I had to actually ask Jay what he needed from me (besides sex, and we'll get to that in just a bit) in order to feel loved—no—*cherished*. I wanted him to feel how much I love him by everyday actions. We all need to feel appreciated. Husbands included.

Turns out, men are not nearly as complicated as busy homeschool moms. (Can't you just hear the angels singing?) A busy

> *If I was going to be That Girl, I needed to get to the heart of what made my husband tick.*

homeschool dad, on even his worst day, does not come close to having the same estrogen-enriched needs of a busy homeschool mom. *We* are women; we like to talk it out at the end of a hard day. More often than not, though, by the time we're done mixing our commentaries with the unique joys and stresses of homeschooling, we've forgotten to pursue, or even include our husbands!

I think on some level, we expect our husbands to be just like us. We assume they want us to show love to them in exactly the way we want them to show love to us. Praise God for His amazing design in making men and women so different!

Simply put, most husbands at their core, are pretty easy to please. For the past twenty years, I have been a student of my husband. Here are a few things that made it to the top of the list of ways to romance your husband—from the perspective of a busy homeschool mom:

1) **Prefer your husband in all things.** Jay is the phone call I take when I think I can't take another call. He is the dinner date I make before I put anything else on the calendar. He is the reason we have white space on our calendar. Our marriage is the priority in our home, and our children know it.

2) **Actively communicate that you respect your husband.** (Respect means a high or special regard.) I fear many women do not grasp the importance of this crucial aspect of the marriage relationship. We communicate respect to our husbands when we trust them to meet our needs; from asking for directions when lost (or not) to providing for our families.

Men tend to have a great need to be respected and the Scriptures are very clear that wives must respect their husbands. The way we behave from day to day with our husbands says a lot about our love for them. When was the last time you told your husband how much you respected him? Here are a few ways you can show him your respect:

• **Verbally:** Try to minimize complaining. Compliment him instead.

• **Physically:** Find out what his top three needs are. Ask your husband what he needs from you in those three areas, and then make a conscious effort to meet those needs. Don't be afraid to ask tough questions—that's how you get to the truth of the matter!

• **Spiritually:** Encourage your husband when you see

him leading your family. If he is not the spiritual leader in your family, pray for him. Talk to him about it in a way that helps him see the importance of his God-given role as the leader in your home.

- **Emotionally:** I've learned that I can respect Jay by recognizing that we are totally different creatures, especially emotionally. Men don't give a lot of weight to feelings. They are more likely to respond to facts. For example, let's say your husband wants to buy a new car. Rather than get upset and become emotional and irrational, write out a budget that clearly explains how much money is needed to meet your expenses each month. Let the facts speak for you, and then respect your husband by allowing him to make that final decision.

3) **Make time.** Remember, your calendar will reflect your priorities. Most busy homeschool moms don't choose curriculum with their husbands in mind. But I'm here to tell you that if your curriculum leaves you cold and exhausted at the end of the day, it's time to find a curriculum that is more suited to helping you put the priority on your marriage.

4) **Be That Girl.** You can do it. Be the girl your husband fell in love with. Were you spontaneous, funny, sexy, and giving towards your husband when he chose you? You still are those things. And even though now you're a busy homeschool mom, he still needs you to be That Girl!

5) **Revisit your romance.** In other words, get back to basics. What is it that makes your husband's eyes light up? Is it a post-it note on the bathroom mirror? Is it an invitation to an intimate rendezvous? Every busy homeschool mom was once a girl who worked to gain the affections of the man she married.

Do you have a vision for bringing romance back into your marriage? If you don't, you should! Ask the Lord to help you be the girl your husband married, and commit yourself to being a student of your husband. If he likes M&M's, put them in his lunch box. If he enjoys basketball, find out what time the game starts. And be there. You'll be amazed at what a difference your efforts to keep the home fires burning will have on your husband.

Remember, you are That Girl!

CHAPTER 3
White Space

PLANNING YOUR LIFE WITH YOUR MARRIAGE IN MIND

Faith goes up the stairs that love has built and looks out the window which hope has opened.
~ Charles Spurgeon

Oh, Elusive Balance

Jay and I have spent many years in full time ministry. We both left Multnomah Bible College (now Multnomah University) with all the energy that our early 20's could offer and just enough inexperience to allow our church schedule to run us over and leave us for dead. Can you relate? You don't have to be a pastor's wife to understand the need for balance. All it really takes to find yourself in a time crunch is a lack of discernment and the propensity towards saying yes to every good thing that comes your way.

Homeschoolers are really prone to becoming unbalanced, because contrary to what we've been hearing for the past thirty years, there really are a lot of things for homeschooling kids (and their parents) to do outside of the home. If you're having panic attacks at the sight of your over-filled calendar, take heart! You're not alone.

> *I am a big believer in having real, transparent relationships with other women.*

Recently, I was enjoying a strawberry smoothie with a dear girlfriend of mine. As we sat out in the afternoon sun, we talked about the time crunches we were experiencing. Hers centered around sports activities for the kids and her husband's busy work schedule. My calendar was just as busy, but for different reasons. With six kids and a growing ministry to run, my life is not your normal schedule either. *By the way*—I am a big believer in having real, transparent relationships with other women. In my experience, grace-filled, godly girlfriends are an absolute must.

Did I mention grace-filled? I love this friend of mine—she laughed because she could never "do" my life and I laughed because I could never "do" hers. Don't you just love that? God knows what we need. As we listened to each other, we also encouraged each other in our relationships with our husbands. She noted that I had mentioned at least three times that I couldn't remember when Jay and I had been out on a date that wasn't business or ministry related. Red flag! She was encouraging me back to a place of balance in my life.

Choices, Changes

Part of the blessing of having a relationship with the Living God in partnership with our husbands is that we get to listen to Him *together*. That relationship also means we get to *choose* how we will spend our time. It's a never-ending series of choices, and each choice has its own end result.

Jay and I are privileged to be able to work together in the ministry God has given us. This has been our heart's desire since we were newly married. Early in 2009, we received the blessing of free office space at a wonderful facility in our hometown of Vancouver, Washington. We knew that having

> *Our choices reveal what we love the most, what we fear, and what is of greatest value to us.*

office space was needed, but we also lost our "perfect commute" when we took that space. It was a choice. It meant that our lives would change, and that we would need to make adjustments if we were going to maintain balance in our home.

Someone once said, "Actions have consequences."

I like to say "Choices mean changes." They do!

> Jesus said, "What does it profit a man if he gains the whole world, and loses his own soul?"
> ~ Mark 8:36, NKJV

Or, in Heidi homeschool paraphrase, "What does it profit a homeschool mom if she homeschools her children and then gets so wrapped up in the busyness of life that she forgets that her primary purpose is to cultivate the hearts and souls of her children for the Kingdom?" The point is, *we get to choose* where we invest our time—just like the man Jesus was talking about in Mark 8:36.

A few years ago, I overheard a conversation at church where one mom was telling another mom that being busy was sinful. I couldn't disagree more. Please understand, I'm not saying it's wrong to be busy. Homeschool moms are busy by nature, like a bee buzzing about its hive. I am busy from the moment my feet hit the floor every morning, just with the daily chores. Add in homeschooling and child-training, and I am one busy homeschool mom!

Life is busy. If you are a homeschool mom, you're even busier. Right? It took a few years of trial-and-error for this busy homeschool mom, but I finally learned something important when my oldest daughter was about twelve years old. I learned that homeschooling demands that I must schedule my time wisely. It makes all the difference!

When I was a new homeschool mom, I bought a book that was all about managing my day. Inside the book, there were some wonderful nuggets of truth about scheduling, but what I found most interesting was the hour-by-hour schedules that the book contained. My head almost exploded just looking at the schedules that some of these homeschool moms keep.

> *Find me a homeschool mom that is not busy and I will show you a mom who is taking a well-deserved nap.*

If you're busy, it's okay. It's normal. Find me a homeschool mom that is not busy and I will show you a mom that is taking a well-deserved afternoon nap. However, if looking at your calendar makes your heart race and your blood pressure rise, it's time to erase some things. You'll need to make some choices about what is most important, first for your marriage, then for your homeschool.

It's time to find some "white space."

White Space

Have you ever heard the Veggie Tales™ song "Busy, Busy?" In it, even an industrious asparagus sings:

> I'm busy, busy, dreadfully busy
> You've no idea what I have to do.
> Busy, busy, shockingly busy
> Much, much too busy for you.

Jay and I laughed until our sides hurt when we first heard this song. We liked to sing the song to each other while we did dishes after dinner and the kids played on the floor at our feet. Obviously, this kind of busy is not the kind you want.

But remember, the problem is not in being busy. The problems come when we find ourselves being busy doing the wrong things. Good things qualify as wrong things, too, did you know that? I have had moments when my calendar was so full of good things that my relationship with my husband suffered. What I discovered is that where there is no "white space" on my calendar, I end up with a roommate instead of a husband.

In order to maintain balance in your home, you need to sit down with your husband and talk about what white space means to him. When I finally sat down with Jay and asked him what his definition of white space was, I was amazed! He thinks of white space as almost any time when we are doing something together. I think of it as totally free, unscheduled time. I feel stressed whenever I look at our calendar and don't see at least two free days in a row. My husband is not so bothered by all we do, so long as we do it together.

> *The problem is not in being busy. The problems come when we find ourselves being busy doing the wrong things.*

We did not have the same needs in this area: basically, Jay wanted more time with me, and I just wanted more unscheduled time. However, facts are facts, and honestly, when my husband and I don't see each other very much, we quarrel. Some people might call it fighting. There, I said it. (Just tryin' to keep it real here, ladies!)

Often, our quarrels would happen because we were both defensive about investing too much of our time separately in other areas of our life. This led to feelings of rejection on both sides. In order to keep this from happening, we sit down and talk about what kind of time we need as a couple and as a family. Turns out that aside from the obvious "alone time," we are happy just being together as a family.

Many nights, our family can be found quietly sitting around the table with our laptops—and that's okay, as long as you understand that those times must be balanced out with real times of sharing, interaction and intimacy (Instant messaging each other doesn't count, by the way. . . unless you're IM'ing an *"invitation"* to your husband!).

A Plan to Prioritize

Here is a list of things that Jay and I do together and as a family to help us keep the stress level at bay and to give more time to each other:

1) We don't sign up for anything unless we can see how it fits into the master calendar. This is because we need to see how it fits into the grand scheme of things. I'm amazed at how fast our calendar fills up. If we don't keep tabs on it, we're doing something every night of the week.

2) We leave plain, unscheduled white space on our calendars to allow for rest and spontaneous "somethings." Spontaneity! Ya gotta have it!

3) We share our meals together most of the time. Here's a funny homeschool fact for you: Most homeschool moms will admit that they don't always grind their own wheat and butcher their own chickens that they raised from an egg on their homestead. It's true! So let yourself off the hook. I think that any meal that is eaten together counts. Even if it's Taco Bell or Marie Callender. (But I won't tell if you won't.)

4) We invest our time in each other. If the kids have a soccer game, then we all make an effort to go. If Jay is leading worship, we're playing in the band. This has helped us to prioritize our activities, because we know that for the most part, it will be a family affair. It's amazing how many things we decide we don't need to do when we look at the impact it will have our beloved white space!

5) We keep our marriage as the priority relationship in our home. For this reason our calendar, reflects both the things that are most important to us, and the priority of our marriage.

Actually, even as I type this, I am thinking of changes we can make to our calendar. We must constantly stay on top of our calendar so that we can make the most of the time we have with our children and as a family.

And as if these were not all good reasons to give your calendar some breathing room, let me give you one more. We have recently noticed that we are no longer in the "growing phase" of our family. Funny, I thought we would be there forever! I am discovering what every busy homeschool mom who has gone before me already knows: The homeschool years go by so fast. Make time to enjoy them!

Keeping your finger on the pulse of your family is your job, busy homeschool mom! If you sense your family's pulse is racing, it might be time to sit down with your husband and see how you can create more white space together.

Chapter 4

VIRTUAL REALITY

The Times, They are a'Changin'

The best things in life . . . aren't things.
~ Art Buchwald

From Toddlers to Term Papers

Do you remember what your life used to be like before you had children? I sure do. Jay and I started dating when we were in college—and we thought life was busy then! However, we always made time for each other, sometimes going to ridiculous lengths to get just a few minutes in before curfew or after work.

Term papers didn't come between us: We studied together. Sickness didn't keep us apart: We sent Cup O' Noodles to the dorms for each other. Even the dormitory curfew couldn't keep Jay and Heidi from using flashlights to send silly messages across the campus parking lot after hours. (Remember, this was before cell phones. And no, I can't believe it either.)

When I think of the lengths we went to just to make sure the other one knew they were loved, it makes me smile. I don't think a day went by in 1989 when my beloved did not express his love to me in some way. I would see him skateboarding across the parking lot and my heart would skip a beat. Oh, how I loved this boy! Yeah, I guess it's fair to say that we were just a couple of kids, but we were crazy about each other. So, in September of 1989, we got married. I was just nineteen.

Remembering this time in our lives gives me such joy! It also serves as a constant reminder that I cannot use the excuse of being a busy homeschool mom when I am putting my needs or our children's needs above our marriage. I mean, seriously! If we could make time then, we can make time now. Truth is, we can make time. Time is a gift. To use it unwisely is to be selfish.

Have you ever noticed that we are the most unkind and selfish with the people we are supposed to love the most? For exam-

> *Time is a gift. To use it unwisely is to be selfish.*

ple, I'm embarrassed to admit that it's easier for me to be rude to one of my children than to a stranger at the grocery store. Why is that? It makes no sense at all! Or does it?

I have a theory about this behavior. I think we give ourselves permission to show the uglier side of our hearts to those with whom our relationships are most secure. For example, a couple that is dating, but hasn't made the big commitment of marriage, had better be on their best behavior if they hope to make it to the altar, right? It's usually not until the couple has been married for a while, and a sense of security has developed, that they allow themselves to treat their spouse as a "given" instead of a *gift*. What a mistake.

It's probably a good thing that young couples in love have no idea of what is in front of them. Truly, I wonder if we would have hesitated, even for a moment, on our wedding day if we had known about the hardships we would face together in

> *I think we give ourselves permission to show the uglier side of our hearts to those with whom our relationships are most secure.*

this life. (And at that time, homeschooling wasn't even part of the deal we made!)

Yes, life is busier now. With six children and a busy, international ministry to homeschoolers to oversee, we face some serious time constraints. Just the other day, Jay and I stole away for lunch together and we marveled at how the time we share together is so precious! It's a commodity we can't afford to waste.

But our culture has its priorities all wrong, and we are wasting precious time each day.

According to the AC Nielsen ratings the average American watches more than four hours of TV each day, or twenty-eight hours per week, which is equivalent to two months of nonstop TV watching every year. I wonder what the statistic would be if, in addition, we could calculate our use of social networking sites like Facebook and Twitter.

My hunch is that we've got our priorities all wrong. I believe we would have healthier, happier marriages if we were more intentional about the way we spent our "free" time.

The Fun, Fear and Folly of the Facebook Generation

Sadly, our hurried and hectic lives probably do the most harm to our marriages. The truth is, we greatly need to spend time alone with our husbands. When we can't find that middle ground of balance between work, homeschool, family and marriage, we are stressed. Our culture demands that we give more and more of our time to things that don't really matter at the end of the day. See if you have given too much of your time to any of these things:

- Social networking sites/Surfing the Internet
- TV
- Church/Ministry
- Work

Instead of being busy investing in things of eternal significance, we busy ourselves by investing in things that are temporary. Sometimes we do it out of ignorance. Other times we use these things as a way to avoid the painful circumstances we find ourselves in. The Internet has become a place for many people to form entirely separate lives from their "real" lives.

In the interest of full-disclosure, I need to tell you that I am a fan of Facebook. I joined Facebook along with my husband some time ago in an effort to keep tabs on our teens who really wanted to be part of the Facebook frenzy. Before long, we found ourselves spending more time there than our kids! It was a blast to reconnect with old friends from high school and college and even more fun to hear how God was working in the lives of hundreds of people who have been part of churches where Jay and I have served over the years.

In this context, sites like Facebook add to life. But there is a caveat to it as well.

Happy, contented people on Facebook can draw boundaries. Throw in a little discontent, and you have a recipe for disaster.

> *Happy, content people on Facebook can draw boundaries. Throw in a little discontent, and you have a recipe for disaster.*

Virtual Reality Comes Home

Unfortunately, the social networking generation has a dark side. If you are struggling in your marriage, please listen to this: Social networking sites like Facebook can become pitfalls for unhappy people. What I mean is if you are unhappy in your marriage, you need to stay off of social networking sites. I am heartbroken by the number of marriages I hear about that are hanging by a thread and are finished off by "chance encounters" online with former lovers or acquaintances.

A few years ago, I was speaking on the topic of marriage to a group of a few hundred homeschool moms. As usual, I encouraged these moms to be real about their lives. To be real is to be honest, not only with your spouse but also with yourself. I never could have imagined what happened next.

"Heidi?"

A young mom I'll call Cindy tapped me on the shoulder. I noticed she was holding a beautiful newborn in her arms. The baby was peacefully sleeping, and the oh-so-familiar look of sleep deprivation in Cindy's eyes softened my heart. I don't know what's worse: sleep deprivation or the pain of childbirth. My heart went out to her.

> *Cindy was expecting her husband to fill that part of her heart that can only be filled by God.*

"Do you have a moment to talk?"

"Sure," I replied. "What's on your mind?" We moved to a quiet spot and she began to tell me her story.

As it turned out, Cindy had come to this homeschool conference in a last-ditch effort to save her marriage. She told me how unhappy she was. She felt chained to the kids, the dishes, the laundry, and her marriage.

Like many homeschool moms, she felt that her husband didn't understand her. They didn't talk like they used to. She felt unappreciated and unloved, at least unloved in the way she had always assumed she would be loved. Cindy was expecting her husband to fill that part of her heart that can only be filled by God.

Naturally, she soon found another way to fill the void that she felt was being left by her husband. She opened a Facebook account and started looking for friends from her past. Like so many other moms caught in the same lie (the lie that Facebook is real) Cindy began to correspond with a boy (I'd call him a man, but that would not be fair) from her high school days.

After three months of late-night conversations and photo exchanges, they had decided to run away together.

I'll be honest, I was angry.

"Lord!" I cried out in my spirit, "What do you want me to say to this mom? I've got nothin'."

I meant it. I didn't have a single thing of worth to share with Cindy.

"Where is your husband?"

"He's down the hall in Jay's workshop," came her sheepish reply. "I am only telling you this because you said we needed to get real. You said we needed to talk to another woman. So I'm getting real. I'm talking to you."

"Of course you are, because I'm safe. What can I do to you?" I thought to myself.

After asking a few more questions, I learned that there was no abuse, no adultery, no wrongful actions on the part of Cindy's husband.

Turns out, Cindy was just married to an ordinary man. Her mom needed to send her home like my mom had sent me home years ago. She needed someone who loved her to tell her the truth about the terrible consequences of adultery. But she didn't want to talk to anyone who would hold her accountable. She hadn't been truly honest with anyone (including herself) for a long time.

Let's face it: Facebook friends are easy. Friendship is hard. MySpace is easy. Marriage is hard.

Cindy had discovered that Facebook friends are easy, but friendship is hard. My Space is easy. Marriage is hard.

Now, instead of a fantasy marriage, Cindy had four kids to raise and a mortgage to pay. It wasn't easy. It was hard. But the truth was right there in black and white. Cindy was just being selfish. And she knew it.

There is nothing special about me. And at that moment, I knew it because I was as empty a vessel as there ever was. My heart cried out to the Lord for some wise word. I didn't know much, but I did know this: God's heart is for the redemption of His people, His love is unending, and His grace knows no limit.

In His mercy, God spoke through me. As I looked at Cindy I suddenly knew exactly what He wanted me to say to His wandering child.

"Cindy?" I looked into her eyes. "Would you mind if I held your baby boy for a moment?"

She looked a little surprised at how our conversation seemed to take this sudden turn, but Cindy carefully placed her gorgeous little baby in my arms. With the authority of that comes from the Spirit, I held that baby and spoke the words that the Lord gave me.

"Cindy, this battle is not about you. You think it is, but the truth is, your heart is far from the Lord. Satan has you right where he wants you, so as far as the spiritual battle for your heart, he thinks it's over. This battle is not for your marriage. You've given up. This is a battle for the heart and mind of the baby that I hold in my arms. This is God's child. If you break the covenant that you have made with your husband, then the Enemy will have a much greater chance of snatching this little one from your arms. He'll do it when you're not looking. He'll use whatever tools he can. Right now, those tools are Facebook and discontent. God has *so much more for you*, if you will just trust Him with your heart."

In just ten minutes, I had been given a glimpse into the life of this precious woman. I prayed with her, and as I handed that beautiful baby boy back to her, I asked her to stay in touch with me. I never heard from her again. Looking back, my heart still aches. I have seen that steely look before. Her eyes were set like flint, and at that point in her life, even the thought of losing the hearts of her four young children did not soften her stance. It's hard to soften a heart that has turned from God—but it's not impossible.

Reality Check

Have you stopped to consider the subtle impact that the media is having on your relationships? If time on the internet, TV, or anything else is taking you away from your first love (Christ) or stealing time from your husband, it's time to rethink your priorities.

Dear Lord,
Help me to be very aware of the time I spend doing things that take me away from my husband and family.
I pray that my spirit would be keenly aware of my motivation for renewing old friendships.
Thank you, Lord, I have Your Spirit inside me.
Help me to listen.
In Jesus Name, Amen.

CHAPTER 5

Homeschool Headache

A COMMON DIAGNOSIS... AND A FEW WAYS TO TREAT IT

All beautiful you are, my darling,
There is no flaw in you.
~ Song of Solomon 4:7

An Important Conversation

Can I call you That Girl? I hope so, because I figure by now you know me pretty well. That being the case, I'm just going to do what I do with all my girlfriends and jump right into one of my favorite subjects: sex. That's right!

I have had some of the best conversations about sex with busy homeschool moms. And it's about time. Sex is one of the most important parts of the marriage relationship, and believe it or not, homeschool moms have a lot to say about it when given the opportunity.

Most people don't think of homeschool moms as women who enjoy wonderful, intimate relationships with their husbands. Saying the words "homeschool" and "mom" together in the same sentence often conjures up images of toddlers and textbooks, not candle-lit bedrooms and romantic evenings of passionate interludes between the sheets.

Being real allows us to have real relationships.

Many of the moms I speak with have told me they don't have time for sex because the children need to be given priority during the homeschool years. Sadly, many wives believe that sex is something that needs very little energy—but I beg to differ. I think that when we start opening our eyes and our hearts to the importance of sex in marriage, there will be a lot more busy homeschool moms talking about it too.

But first things first: We need to get real with each other and ask God to give us His perspective.

Getting real can be challenging. As I said earlier, it means laying aside the facade we so easily put up for others. As hard as it is to admit we don't have it all together, it's also very freeing. Something wonderful happens when we're not trying to be someone we're not. We become more open to hearing God's still, small voice. We can also hear the voices of godly men and women who we trust to speak into our lives. Being real allows us to have real relationships.

If you have to pretend around your friends, then you've got a problem. Nurture the relationships in your life that allow you (and the other person) to be exactly who you are, flaws and all. Bear with one another (Colossians 3:13). Allow yourself to be vulnerable. That's when you'll start to find That Girl again.

Homeschool Headache

Have you ever had a homeschool headache? I have. There have been times at the end of the day when I just knew that if one more person asked me for one more thing, something ugly was going to happen. I know that every busy homeschool mom reading this right now is nodding in agreement because let's be honest. Sometimes, sex is the last thing on our minds. Okay, maybe "sometimes" is being too generous. I get it. Lack of sleep, stress within the marriage, financial pressures—these are serious libido killers.

Funny thing though, my husband seriously never feels this way. Sex is *never* the last thing on his mind. It's not always the first thing either, but in twenty years, I have never seen it be the *last* thing. We have often looked at each other at the end of the day and our eyes say it all. They just don't always say the same thing!

Now, before you get ready for me to quote familiar verses about how your body doesn't belong to you (and by the way, it doesn't), I want to steer you in a different direction. I want you to look at sex as the amazing thing God intended his children to see it as. Truth is, God thinks sex is awesome. (It was His idea, after all!) Sex is everywhere in God's creation. In fact, last year when I was teaching botany in our homeschool, we discovered that there are actually ferns that reproduce using that old familiar "sperm meets egg" scenario. Can you imagine? I'm not kidding! You're a homeschool mom—you might want to look it up. My point is that if God thinks sex is a good idea, we should, too!

A Different Perspective on a Familiar Verse

Several years ago, I was preparing to speak at a women's conference in Oregon. We were talking about self-image—

learning how to see ourselves as God sees us, instead of how the world sees us. As I studied some passages, I came across Proverbs 5:18.

Before I went any further in my study, I read the verse to Jay. The interesting conversation that ensued went something like this:

> **Heidi:** Check this verse out, Jay. [reads with sarcasm] "May your fountain be blessed, and may you rejoice in the wife of your youth."
> *Of course* you are supposed to rejoice in the wife of your youth! Because let's be honest! In a few years, the wife of your youth will be only a distant memory of the wife you have now—things will be sagging, her hair will lose its youthful shine, and Oil of Olay will be the one thing she can't live without. She'll be old and tired! You had better rejoice in the wife of your youth because when she's old there won't be much to rejoice about!
> **Jay:** Wow, babe, you need to stop reading *People*. That's not how I see that verse at all!

When I read this verse, I can envision an old man sitting on the porch with the wife of his youth—you know—the one God gave to him when he was young! The man is looking at this beautiful old woman, and just remembering the *wife of his youth* makes him smile.

Heidi: [climbs down out of her tree] Oh. I would never have thought of it that way.

Just hearing Jay's take on this verse made me wonder how my other girlfriends would read it. So I read it at the retreat and wouldn't you know it? Almost all of the moms saw that verse the same way that I did! Most of the women I talk to are very self-conscious about their bodies. And why shouldn't they be? We live a culture that is literally consumed with sex and body image. All you have to do is go through the checkout stand at the grocery store to see pictures of "fat" women. We all know that according to our culture, "fat" is defined as anyone who is over a size 6 and who has (gasp!) cellulite.

In the name of beauty, women in the today's culture undergo liposuction, breast augmentation, tummy tucks, face lifts, eye lifts, and even chin implants. Instead of being seen as a sign of wisdom, wrinkles send 40-somethings running for Botox injections. I'm not suggesting that these things are sinful, but what I am saying is we have a serious problem in our culture. We have bought into the lie that *People Magazine* knows more about beauty than God does. It's just not true.

God's word is so counter-cultural! The Bible tells us that God is not focused on the outward things; rather, He is ultimately concerned with the condition of our hearts. Look at what Samuel said:

> "The Lord does not look at the things man looks at.
> Man looks at the outward appearance,
> but the Lord looks at the heart."
>
> ~ 1 Samuel 16:7

Whose Body Image?

We have God's Word and yet we defer to the wisdom of the world to define how our physical bodies should look. The effects of this are found in nearly every home in America. Homeschool moms are not immune, either. See if you have had any of these thoughts run through your mind:

- The body I had at twenty was more beautiful than the body I have now.
- My husband misses the way I used to look.
- If I were thinner, I would be more attractive.
- My (fill-in-the-blank) is too big/small/wide/narrow.
- My hips are too curvy.
- My breasts are ruined from breast-feeding!

I bet I am not alone when I say that I have struggled with these things. With each pregnancy, I could hear that nagging voice in my head reminding me that I would never have the body of That Girl again. I wanted to be intimate with my husband, but even in my early twenties, I began to feel insecure. It took a lot of courage for me to admit my insecurities to my husband. Praise God, those fears turned out to be unfounded, and I learned something amazing about the way my husband sees me as a woman (not a homeschool mom). Turns out, my husband loves me. My imperfect body is of much more concern to me that it ever was to him! I had bought the lie.

And what a lie it is. Straight from the father of lies.

Most women are very aware of the flaws in their bodies,

and in many cases it keeps them from being intimate with their husbands in the way that God intended. When I finally stopped listening to the lies of the Enemy and looked at myself through the eyes of my husband, I no longer saw a busy homeschool mom, I began to see myself as God made me.

It wasn't easy. Looking at myself with new eyes meant that I had to face the fact that I had brought some of my body issues on myself, because I had chosen to believe the world's definition of beauty instead of God's. Even when I had a "perfect" (or at least pre-pregnancy) body, I was insecure. That insecurity affected my relationship with my husband. As a young wife, I didn't realize that one day, I would miss that flat, un-stretched-out tummy, and instead of enjoying my body and sharing it unashamedly with my husband, I lamented about various flaws I saw.

> *Most women are very aware of the flaws in their bodies, and in many cases it keeps them from being intimate with their husbands in the way God intended.*

The point is that God gave your body to you! Before I go any further, I want to make something clear: Your husband doesn't need for your body to be perfect. I was surprised to find that my husband didn't notice the things that made me want to cover myself up in a flannel nightgown every night—he just wanted to be with That Girl!

Yes, he wanted me to be That Girl in bed, in the same way that I wanted to find her there again. Enjoy the body God has given you, busy homeschool mom, flaws and all. Take care of yourself. When you are 85, you will be wishing for the body you have right now and there will be no going back.

The Husband of Her Youth

My grandmother was amazing. She was married to Grandpa for nearly 75 years. She's been home with the Lord for a while now, but the lessons I learned about marriage from her will stay with me forever. In the last few years of their lives together, my grandparents lived in an assisted living facility in Portland, Oregon. One afternoon, I was talking with Grandma and she stopped mid-sentence and glanced over at Grandpa, who was sitting in a recliner next to her. She sighed.

"When did I get old, Heidi?" she asked. "Inside, I feel like the girl that Grandpa courted in Fairbury. I look at Grandpa and even now, I just want to run into his arms. He had such strong arms, Heidi. Isn't he just the most handsome man? When did we turn 90? When did I get old?"

I studied her eyes. She clearly missed the physical connection that they used to share. Even as a child, I recognized it—Grandpa never made a secret of the fact that he thought Grandma was beautiful! We loved to watch him chase her all over the house.

Time takes no prisoners, however, and now their lives bore little resemblance to those days. We talked for a while longer. I was surprised at how clear her memories of Grandpa were. As a tear ran down her sweet face, I held her hand in mine and silently thanked God for my husband. Time goes by so fast. A thousand memories of my grandparents washed over me at that moment and I realized that Grandma was still absolutely in love with Grandpa. I was privileged to hear her *remember the husband of her youth.*

> *Busy homeschool mom, you are That Girl.*
>
> *You are the wife of your husband's youth.*

Busy homeschool mom, you are That Girl. You *are* the wife of your husband's youth. Being a homeschool mom makes your role that much more exciting—because a million memories from now, Lord willing, you will be able to look back at your romance and smile about the times that you persevered through the homeschool years. Are you enjoying each other as God intended? If not, keep reading. You might be in the vortex.

Life in the Homeschool Vortex

Some of you reading this book are living in the homeschool vortex and you don't even know it. (Just because you don't wear a jumper doesn't mean you haven't slipped in.) The vortex is a lot like the pit that King David talks about in Psalm 40. Let's take a brief look at the first part of that Psalm.

> I waited patiently for the Lord to help me,
> and He turned to me and heard my cry.

(Can you relate? David goes on...)

> He lifted me out of the pit of despair
> Out of the mud and the mire.

Now, this sounds like the homeschool vortex to me. A pit of despair. In the homeschool vortex, we wonder why we started homeschooling—if we can even do it—let alone nurture our husband and teach our kids! Praise God for giving us His Word! It's literally filled with examples of real human beings just like me who struggle with everyday issues. But be careful, because after a while, those "issues" can put us into a pit—or the homeschool vortex. Same thing.

In the final analysis, it doesn't matter how you get into the vortex—it only matters that you recognize you're in so that you can get out.

Do you long for intimacy with your husband? There are a several indicators that I have learned to look for that help me to discern where our marriage is at when it comes to sex:

You might be in the vortex if:

- Your bedroom is filled with homeschool magazines and laundry
- You have lost your desire for sex
- Flannel is your primary love language in bed
- You consider grading math papers priority over sex

- You're too tired for sex
- You think sex is just for making babies
- Pornography has entered your marriage in any way

Excuses Are Like Elbows . . .

My dad used to say, "Excuses are like elbows—everybody's got them." Many busy homeschool moms are using the excuse of homeschooling to ignore the sexual needs of their husbands. I have to be honest. That's not okay. In fact, it's sin. Look around you. Sex is powerful thing. If it weren't, the porn industry, which breaks up literally thousands of marriages each year, would not be thriving. If sex were not powerful, David would not have murdered Uriah in order to take his wife.

According to most experts, your husband thinks about sex all the time. In our culture, men are visually assaulted at every turn by erotic images that compete for his attention—on TV, at the grocery store, and at your local Borders Bookstore. Sex is everywhere.

When you use any excuse—with the exception of abuse—to avoid sex, not only are you disobeying God's word, you are *missing out* on one of the best parts of married life and you are misunderstanding the importance of sex in marriage.

To ignore the sexual needs of your husband or to reject his advances is to tear at the fabric of who you are as a couple. Don't be fooled into thinking sex doesn't matter. It does. Neglect this part of your marriage and you will suffer devastating results.

Homeschooling is hard work. I don't know very many homeschool moms who have an a ton of extra energy left over at the end of the day. (Though I have met a few!) It's not wrong to pour our lives out for our family. But at the end of the day, if you are putting the kids and homeschooling above your husband, you need to take a good, long look at how things got to where they are now.

Making Your Bedroom a Retreat

Has your bedroom become a multi-purpose room?

It has, if :

- You store homeschool materials in it
- You have kids (not infants) sleeping in your room
- The desktop computer is in your room
- You have laundry piles on your bed
- You feel stressed instead of refreshed when you enter your room

A long time ago, a wise woman whom I had come to look to as a mentor, let me in on one of the secrets to the thirty-plus years of romance she had shared with her husband.

She had young children, and her house was not immaculate (part of why I love her so much), but I am telling you, this couple's bedroom was an absolute haven.

What does your bedroom say about your marriage?

She accomplished this on a pastor's salary, but it looked like no expense had been spared. Just walking into that room inspired me to be a better wife! Beautiful curtains hung over the windows; the room was un-cluttered; candles adorned the dresser; garage sale finds became beautiful wall hangings; pillows of every shape were beautifully arranged on their full-size bed. Nothing was left out—from the smell of the potpourri that simmered in the corner on a night stand to the restful color of the walls, this room was a romantic retreat.

My friend understood the power and the *promise* of the sexual relationship and she intended to be the place where her husband yearned to come home to at the end of the day. What does your bedroom say about your marriage? You don't have to spend a lot of money to create a restful place for the two of you to be alone together. The effort alone will speak volumes to your husband about your love for him and it will demonstrate in a very tangible way that you love him.

Not sure where to begin? Start with clearing the clutter and go from there. A little effort now will have a huge payoff later. I like to say it's the "gift that keeps on giving!"

Desire

For most husbands, the greatest pleasure he has in his life is the physical relationship he shares with his wife. The Bible speaks about the sexual relationship as a mystery, though, and I have often found myself thinking that the real mystery is why women can't seem to get as excited about this part of married life as men.

It's important to note that desire doesn't always mean having sex.

As a busy homeschool mom myself, I get it. I'm not here to make you feel bad for your lack of desire. In truth, it's important to note that desire doesn't always mean having sex, but it does mean that you let your husband know you do want him, and not just because he's good around the house! If we are going to keep the home fires burning, we need to get real about what is going on inside our relationships and focus like a laser beam on every aspect of married life.

Do you remember my story about the game I used to play in elementary school where the boys chased the girls? I really believe that's how we're wired. But just like in third grade, there is a point in time in which your boy wants to be pursued by you. He wants to know that you *desire* him physically. I don't think I've ever seen my husband with a bigger smile on his face than the times I have planned a special romantic evening for him.

When I show Jay I desire him above all others and back that up by enjoying him in the way that God intended for husbands and wives to enjoy one another, he is a happy homeschool dad. It's funny, I told him one time that I feel that way when he does dishes without being asked. We're just wired differently.

If you are struggling with a persistent lack of desire, I encourage you to make an effort to do something about it, even if it takes you out of your "comfort zone." Talk to your husband about it. It may be an issue you can address with your doctor, or it may be something that you need to work through with someone you trust such as a counselor, pastor, sister or best friend. One thing is for sure: If you ignore this vital part of your relationship, your marriage will suffer.

All I Want to Do Is Sleep!

Are you tired? I sure am. And it's not just because I'm a busy homeschool mom. It's motherhood in general. I don't know about you, but having six children has turned me into a night owl.

At our house, nighttime is the only time of the day when the house is quiet and I feel like I can think straight! I like to blame it on the kids. In fact, it's late as I'm writing right now! The strangest thing happens to me when the house is quiet—I can start to feel like my old self again. It's the time I like to prepare for the next day, write the proverbial "to do" lists and maybe read a book. Okay, or get on Facebook. (Just trying to keep it real.)

However, there have been many times in the evening when I have just sat down to relax and I hear "Coming to bed?" from down the hall. I have to admit, I have occasionally thought to myself, "Sure I am! After you're asleep!" In fact, when our children were babies, this was a real struggle for me. It can be particularly difficult when babies are little. If you are a nursing mother right now and your baby is four months or younger, you have my unwavering understanding! But don't take your eyes off what's most important.

One of Satan's most effective weapons is simple: to create separateness between a husband and wife. He'll do it however he can and sex is a great area in which to create a chasm between a husband and wife. Whether it's poor scheduling or poor prioritizing, anytime I notice that we are at odds with each other—if I step back and look at the "big picture" of our life—I will usually find that we are simply not spending enough time together.

If you are too tired for sex, it's time to make some changes. Affection and conversation seem to come more easily (as I've told many a busy homeschool mom before) when I have my priorities in line and I save the best part of me for my husband.

As a matter of fact, I usually say, "Why don't we do this more often?" That's just how forgetful I am.

Sex Is About More Than Making Babies

Certainly it was within God's creative ability to make procreation a dull, necessary part of making sure the human race continued. Instead, He gave us the ability to enjoy sex for the sake of enjoyment alone.

Did anyone ever tell you that sex was only for making babies? I hope you realize how far from God's heart that is. God's heart is that you enjoy sex with your husband. His design is infinitely more wonderful and loving toward us that we can ever comprehend.

> "For this reason a man will leave his father and mother and be united to his wife, and they will become one flesh."
>
> ~ Genesis 2:24

I love the imagery of Scripture. One flesh. The language itself suggests intensity, infusion and pleasure. It also shows God's heart in uniting a man and wife in this way. God *wants* us to be *one flesh*. Just think about that with me for a moment. God did not say, "For this reason, a man will leave his parents and they will have babies." He said, we would leave our parents and cleave to our spouse, and become one flesh.

Sex is about so much more than making babies. I truly believe that God meant for sex to provide us with respite from the stresses of this world. A healthy sexual relationship serves to strengthen the bonds between a husband and wife. Sex gives physical pleasure and release. And, wonder of wonders, the most amazing thing we know of happens through sex; new life is created. Every time I think of this amazing gift, I am speechless.

The Gift of Choosing Again

Homeschool mom, when you chose to marry your husband, you were choosing to make him your first priority in all things. I want to challenge you to choose your husband *again*. Choose him first. The best homeschooling and the best mothering is borne out of an overflow of a strong, committed marriage. Loving your husband is a choice. Seeing him as God's gift to you is a powerful thing.

Every day that you share with the husband of your youth is a day that you can choose to love him with the kind of passion that God meant for you to enjoy. In fact, I wonder—when was the last time you told your husband that you would choose him all over again? Choose to be *That Girl* again. Choose to see yourself as the girl that chose to marry your husband.

I want to encourage you to choose to love freely and openly. Let your husband know that you desire him. Choose to turn a deaf ear to the lies of the Enemy and see yourself as God sees you—and then, let the "naked and unashamed" experience begin anew.

CHAPTER 6

Being Naked

THE HEART OF COMMUNICATION IN MARRIAGE

Eros will have naked bodies;
Friendship naked personalities.
~ C.S. Lewis

Boiling It Down

Communication seems simple, but clearly we still have a lot to learn about it.

Communication workshops abound. Marriage seminars focus on communication. Thousands of books have been written on the subject. I questioned whether or not to write about this subject at all, because it's ubiquitous and yet so complex, and then it hit me: Communication isn't that hard when you boil it down to basic root issues.

I have come to believe that talking about communication

styles, et cetera, without talking about the heart of communication is like talking about the lighting or contrast in a photograph, but ignoring the person in it. Let's look for a few minutes at what the Bible says about communication.

In Paul's letter to the Philippians, he said, "Do nothing out of selfish ambition or vain conceit, but in humility consider others better than yourselves. Each of you should look not only to your own interests, but also to the interests of others." (Philippians 2:2-3)

What would our marriages look like if each of us considered the other person in our marriage as better than ourselves? I'm convinced that if we were to put this one simple truth into practice within our marriages, we would see transformation from the inside out.

Why? It's simple: We can learn helpful communication skills, but if we lack the heart of Christ when we speak, the Bible says we sound like a gong. Ouch.

I'm not going to spend a bunch of time talking about assertive, passive, passive-aggressive or non-defensive styles of communication. Instead, let's look for a few minutes at what the Bible says about communication. In marriage, more than in any other relationship, we have to get this right.

On Being "Naked"

Have you ever bared your most personal thoughts to someone and then instinctively recognized that you had made a mistake? Maybe it was the upturned eyebrow, or the look of disappointment in the other person's eyes. Sometimes the result of our "naked" communication is outright rejection. Either way, it hurts and it can hurt to the point of shriveling your soul.

Marriage is the one relationship we enter into that requires a "nakedness of spirit." True, honest communication requires that both parties trust each other with their deepest, most personal thoughts and emotions.

That means our marriages need to be safe places.

It also requires absolute trust in the person you are talking with. In marriage, husbands and wives must have the best interest of the other person at heart. This requires pure motives. I love the quote from C.S. Lewis at the beginning of this chapter; true friendship really does require that we have "naked personalities" and a good friendship is the core of a successful marriage.

Are you a trustworthy confidant for your husband? If your husband is to be your best friend, then you must be able to be as naked with each other in your conversations as you are in bed.

When I thought about what being naked in my personality meant and what it meant for my marriage, the first word that came to mind was "risk." Every good relationship involves a certain amount of risk.

My dear friends, the Lamberts, have often said that "love" is really spelled R-I-S-K because that's what true love does. It risks everything for the chance to be truly known and to know the other person.

But while we risk something when we share our deepest thoughts with another human being, the risk pales in comparison to the importance of the motivation of our heart in the marriage relationship. At the end of the day, it is the motives of the heart that determine the outcome of most conversations we have.

Sure, it sounds easy enough, but when we take an honest look at ourselves, we find that often times we are motivated not by love, but by selfishness.

Listening and Hearing Are Not the Same Thing

Several years ago, we were sitting in the living room of a fellow pastor from Mount Vernon. We were sharing stories of God's work in our hearts and of mistakes we had made in ministry. As it turns out, we seem to learn more from our mistakes than we do from our successes. As we related with each other, our conversation turned to lessons we had learned through communication debacles with other brothers and sisters in Christ.

I had to laugh at the similarities between poor communication in friendships and poor communication inside our marriage. Jay and I learned early on in our marriage that if we didn't really take the time to listen to the other person, our conversations only got us further in trouble.

Sound familiar?

Several years ago, Jay and I started being very intentional about the way we communicated with each other. We started repeating what we thought we had heard the other person say when we disagreed. We were both amazed at how many times we did not really understand the other person!

Half the time, I heard Jay, but I had not understood what he was trying to say. I heard him, but I wasn't listening to him. Repeating what I *thought* he had said proved to be a very useful tool in our marriage. It also revealed how different we were in how we perceived the other person!

Tact and Timing

One night, we were sharing ministry mishaps with a friend and his wife. "It's all about tact and timing," Bill said. He was right. The Bible says basically the same thing in Proverbs 25:11. "Right words spoken in the right time are like apples of gold in a silver setting."

If you're frustrated with your husband, take the time to really think about when you should approach him to talk about it. I can promise you, the time to criticize your husband is not when he walks in the door after a hard day at work. If he is struggling with something that is already weighty, consider whether or not you need to bring up another difficult topic or if you can bear with him for a little while longer.

Often times, when I have taken the time to ask the Lord about something that is bothering me before I take it to my husband. He soothes my hurt in a way that covers both my part in that frustration and also my husband's.

The fact is, even if your words are true, if you approach each other at the wrong time, your words will sting instead of soothe. If your motive is to bring healing and understanding, then timing really is everything. Oh, how we need discernment for the right time when we speak the right words with our beloved.

Busy Homeschool Moms Summary on Communication

Tact and timing. Preferring one another. Bearing with each other. God's word can be mined for nugget after nugget of truth about the heart of communication. So often we wound each other unnecessarily when a visit with Lord would reveal a much better way to communicate with our husband.

Colossians 3:13 says, "Bear with each other and forgive whatever grievances you may have against one another. Forgive as the Lord forgave you." Now you tell me, what kind of a husband would not respond to that kind of forgiveness? Bearing with one another means that we look past bad moods, bad days, and PMS to see the bigger picture. In marriage, the bigger picture involves passing on a legacy of love and respect to our children and grandchildren.

The fact is, even if your words are true, if you approach each other at the wrong time, your words will sting instead of soothe.

I'm trying to pass that legacy on to our children by being my husband's biggest fan. They know at the end of the day, Mom and Dad love each other. We don't always act in the best way that we could, but we always come back to the bigger picture. That means we prefer one another.

When We Disagree

We've all heard the amazing story of Esther. In fact, her story is so incredible, an entire book of the Old Testament is devoted to it. Allow me to summarize.

Esther, a Jew, was married to a Persian king named Ahasuerus (no, I can't pronounce it either) who had signed a decree to have all the Jews killed. Because of this, Esther was in a unique and life-threatening situation. Her very life, and the lives of her people, demanded that she interact with her husband with a great deal of courage and wisdom.

Keep in mind, the king didn't know that Esther was a Jew. He only knew she was absolutely stunningly beautiful (Apparently, that was all he needed to know, as his first wife, Queen Vashti, was said to have been the most beautiful woman in all Persia). However, being married to the king of Persia didn't give Esther much protection. If she displeased him, it was very likely that she would either be divorced, like the king's first wife or even worse she could be killed. It was serious business to upset or even displease the king.

Obviously, this is "Extreme Wife 101" right here, which is why I find it so amazing. The future of the Jewish people literally hung on how well Esther communicated with her husband! Esther knew in her heart that what the king was going to do was wrong. Her heart ached when she realized that she was in disagreement with her husband. We also know that she was very aware of the king's authority and her place in it.

Praise the Lord for His Word! As we read this account, we find that Esther's response has provided us with a beautiful, biblical model for how to approach a husband who might be making a decision that we feel is wrong before the Lord.

Wait, then Wait Some More

In Esther 4:16, we see that the first thing she did was to gather her maidservants and begin to fast and pray (I know, I know, you are tired of hearing about these women in the Bible and all their maidservants. I feel your pain on that one.). Anyway, I love Esther's response because it's so counter intuitive to what our sin nature wants to do. I don't know about you but I struggle to make prayer my first response to most things. My first response when my husband and I disagree is usually to try and win him over with my good argument. According to the Bible, though, that's not the best response. God wants our response to be three things for sure:

- motivated by love (1 Corinthians 16:14)
- bathed in prayer (1 Thessalonians 5:17)
- gentle (Ephesians 4:2)

Something else stands out about the way Esther approached this situation. She waited for the Lord. She *really* waited. Even when Esther's husband asked her to share what was on her mind, she waited another day! Can you imagine the burden she was carrying? And yet, she waited on the Lord. I wonder what our marriages would look like if we learned to put Esther's example into practice in our everyday lives. Waiting patiently upon the Lord requires that we are listening to Him above all other things.

As you know, it turned out that waiting on the Lord and seeking His will above all else was the right move for Esther. Her actions were motivated by love, bathed in prayer, and combined with a gentle, sincere respect for her husband. Ultimately, her willingness to set aside her needs for the needs of others saved the Jewish people from certain death.

Insight from Esther's Example

We can learn so much from Esther's story. When I read her story again, I noticed a few things that every busy homeschool mom should be putting into practice.

First, Esther showed that *she respected her husband.* She did not try to get her way through manipulation, but wisely asked God to show her how to approach her husband. Esther didn't gossip with her maidservants about how worried she was about her husband's decision-making abilities. She took those concerns to the Lord.

Second, Esther had demonstrated that *she was trustworthy.* Her husband trusted what she said and he demonstrated his love for her as he listened to her. She had won not only his physical affection, but his listening ear. He knew that he was safe with her. By the way, Esther did what women have been doing for their men since the dawn of time. She cooked for him before she shared what was on her mind. (There really *is* nothing new under the sun!)

Last, *she was a student of her husband.* She learned a lot, I'm sure, from Queen Vashti's previous mistakes, but remember, Esther was motivated by love. She was carrying the weight of a nation on her shoulders. It was not only in her best interest to learn how to best communicate with her husband, it was in the best interest of an entire nation!

Seeing the Bigger Picture

We don't often think of how important it is that we learn to communicate lovingly and effectively with our husbands. After all, we don't have an entire nation depending on whether or not we get this "marriage thing" right. Or do we?

I truly believe that if we could only see into the future, we would see that an entire nation *is* depending on it. If we could stop and look at the affects of the mentoring and discipling of our children, we might see amazing changes in our culture. Perhaps we would find that many families could be spared from the devastation of divorce.

Esther's actions were motivated by love, bathed in prayer, and combined with a gentle, sincere respect for her husband.

If we were to truly love our husbands with our words and then match those words with our actions, I wonder how many generations of children might enter into marriages of their own with a right perspective. We must not underestimate the power of communicating with our husband.

More Than Lip Service

I cringe when I think of all the thoughtless, even unkind, things I have said to my husband over the years. I have corrected him, interrupted him, spoken over him—yep. I'm just that amazing as a wife. Praise God, His mercies toward me are new every single morning! (Come to think of it, Jay's mercies have been new to me each morning as well.) God has given me the opportunity to learn from my mistakes, as well as a husband who patiently walks beside me and trusts that I love him, even when I don't communicate that love to him as I should.

The bottom line in communication is not style. To get style down and miss the heart of communication is literally giving your marriage nothing more than "lip service!" Your marriage is a ministry. As a woman of God, you are on a mission in your marriage. Do you realize your marriage is an opportunity for you to grow in your walk with God? When we realize that our willingness to minister unconditionally to our husbands is part of successful communication, we have found the best place to start.

Communication Frustration

Sometimes, we just need to start again. So many wives have told me that no matter what they do, their husbands simply will not communicate with them. If this is you, I want to encourage you to read the book of Esther. Commit the situation with your husband to prayer. Ask God to help you communicate *love* to your husband, and ask Him to show you how you can relate to him in a healthy, Christ-honoring way.

No, it's not always easy, but the sacrifice will be worth it. One more thing: It's okay—in fact, it's good—to ask for help from others around you. If you're struggling in your marriage, get real about it. Even if it is the most difficult thing you have ever done.

Busy homeschool mom, your commitment to good communication with your husband will speak volumes to him. You do NOT need to constantly remind your husband that he is not a good communicator. I'm not suggesting you not talk with him, quite the contrary! What I am suggesting is that you make Proverbs 25:11 the communication creed in your home.

> "Right words spoken in the right time are like apples of gold in a silver setting."
>
> ~Proverbs 25:11

Instead of complaining, be That Girl. You might just be amazed by the changes you will see over time . . . over time . . . over time. Did I mention it takes time?

Remember too, that we're modeling marriage for our children. Our children will learn from us how to communicate (or, how not to) with wisdom and love in their own marriages. If we educate our children in the academics but fail to live out the principles that are laid out in God's word in our marriages, we will have missed the most amazing part about homeschooling. That opportunity—the greatest benefit to Christian homeschooling—is discipleship.

Pass it on.

CHAPTER 7

Parallel Lives

PARTNERING ON PURPOSE

"See you in twelve years"
Homeschool Dad to his wife on her first day
homeschooling their kindergartner

Am I Normal?

Do you ever wonder what life is like for other homeschooling families? When I was brand new to homeschooling, the first thing I did was go to the library and devour every book that offered insight into the ways that other homeschoolers spent their days. I needed to understand how I could home educate our children and stay sane. Are you with me?

It was fascinating reading. Turns out there are many kinds of homeschoolers. (So much for typical stereotypes.) Some were homesteaders with chickens and goats; some were classically educating; some were doing unit studies. I was riveted! Seriously!

But at the end of the books, I still did not have my answer. Yes, I cared about the different homeschooling styles, but what I really wanted to know was *how do homeschooling moms get it all done? What is normal?* I couldn't conceive of getting along with my children all day long, much less being responsible for their education. I had a lot to learn, and, unfortunately, I only knew a few homeschooling moms back in 1998.

For a moment, I considered stalking the ones I did know—you know—in a friendly sort of way just to get a peek into their lives. But my husband convinced me that I was better off to take a "trial and error" approach. God has a funny way of bringing us around to His way of doing things.

Turns out that God wanted me to learn how to homeschool by listening to His still, small voice. Trouble was, I couldn't seem to find a moment of quiet in which to hear it!

Have you ever felt like that?

Each Day Is an Opportunity. . . For something

Mondays can really lay me flat. Whenever Monday goes wrong it's easy for me to feel as if I have set the tone for the rest of the week. See if you can't relate to "one of those days:"

7:00 a.m. Alarm goes off (or a baby "goes off"). I keep thinking, "Just five more minutes," and I oversleep. I hate that. For all you 5 a.m.'ers, my hat's off to you. I don't know how you do it.

Like most busy homeschool moms, as soon as my feet hit the floor in the morning, I am running. And I don't necessarily mean frantically, I'm just busy. Chores begin. There is laundry to start, breakfast to set out, beds to make, and kids to dress.

8:00 a.m. Phone usually starts ringing. If I am not on top of my day by that time, it is likely that one of the kids will embarrass me and answer the phone in my place. Inevitably, the message that I am either in the shower or in the bathroom will be relayed to the caller. (I *really* hate that.)

9:00 a.m. School is in full swing by now, toddler needs attention. Stop school. Find sippy cup.

9:10 a.m. Find 8 year-old boy and re-instruct him on his math assignment.

9:15 a.m. Repeat.

10:00 a.m. Take oldest child to Biology class at the co-op, all the while thanking God that I am not dissecting a cow's eyeball on my kitchen counter this year. Get halfway there only to hear an announcement about the notebook being in Dad's car.

10:15 a.m. Call Jay. Arrange to meet him at a mutually agreeable location. Swap books. Exchange longing glances. Get back into the car.

11:00 a.m. Check in with 6-year old daughter, who could literally use up every spare moment of my time if I had it to give. Go over reading lesson, which is interrupted by a phone call from another busy homeschool mom who needs a little encouragement. Take the call. Try not to feel guilty.

1:30 p.m. Start reading with 6-year old again.

1:46 p.m. Remember that I need to feed the family dinner at some point. Daydream about the maidservants that Esther had at her disposal.

3:30 p.m. Double check that all school assignments given to the three oldest children are at least mostly done. Take three youngest children to the dentist.

5:30 p.m. Drive-thru McDonald's on the way home from the dentist. Give brief-but-powerful lecture about the merit of apple slices over French fries.

6:00 p.m. Jay arrives home from work. Serve dinner on paper plates. Ten year old decides it should be a "romantic" night. He lights candles and dims lights. Dad says he can't see his hamburger. Lights go back up.

7:00 p.m. Put little ones in the bathtub while older ones clean the kitchen.

8:00 p.m. Run a load of laundry. Tuck two kids into bed.

8:30 p.m. Call Mom for a visit. Notice how quiet things are at her house.

9:00 p.m. Sit with my husband and ask him how his day was. Remind him that I really need to get up at 7:00 a.m. if I am going to be any good at this "homeschooling thing." He reminds me that I need to go to bed earlier for that to be a reality.

10:00 p.m. Determine that tomorrow will be much more organized. Make schedule, plan menu, create shopping list. Set out schoolwork for the next day.

11:00 p.m. Triumphantly announce to my husband that I have "figured it out" and wait for his approving smile, which he gives. Teens come upstairs and ask a question that is more complicated than I can possibly comprehend at 11 p.m. I think it involves other teens and a weekend event. I can't be sure.

11:30 p.m. Notice the time. Just as we are getting ready to turn out the lights, we remember the longing glances we exchanged in the parking lot at 10:15 that morning. Glance at the clock. Briefly discuss a plan for the next night that gives us more than 30 minutes of "quality" time.

11:35 p.m. Try to sleep instead of calculating the number of hours I have left to actually rest.

Sound familiar? Now granted, this is not every day at our house, but with six kids and an active ministry, it's been exactly this way on more than one occasion! Life is just busy. Like I said before though, it's not "busy" that's the problem.

Slow Fade

The problem is parallel living. The problems begin when the busy homeschool mom's life becomes "all homeschooling all the time" and her husband's life is centered fully around his job. He does his thing, she does hers.

Slowly, the couple loses the sense of wonder and intimacy that God has designed them to enjoy.

It happens so gradually that most of the time, we don't even see it until we're way off course. We roll along in our daily lives, going from one responsibility to another until one day, we discover that we don't really know what's going on in the life of the person we committed to loving for the rest of our lives.

A closer look reveals that we're living more like college roommates than husband and wife. If you think I'm kidding,

I'm not. This scenario is playing out in families everywhere these days.

Does this strike a chord with you? If it does, keep reading, because this is important stuff. When we live **parallel lives with our husbands, we are a lot like that proverbial frog in the pot of warm water. Better to know the "heat is on" before the pot starts boiling.**

And just in case you're wondering . . . the heat is on.

Parallel living

Have you ever looked at parallel lines? They run alongside each other, exactly the same distance apart, for their entire existence. **Perfect parallel lines never cross, because there is never any difference in degree of the space between the lines. You may think it's just math, but take a close look at the parallel line image.**

In marriage, parallel lives are what happen to a husband and his wife when their lives do not intersect. But life rarely goes along mathematical lines. We tend to have our ups and downs. If you take those two parallel lines and put even the smallest degree of separation between them, you will find that not too far down the road, they will be so far apart from each other they can no longer even see one another! One permanent degree of separation, one way or the other, and you've got disaster in a marriage.

That's Just the Way It Is

A few years ago, I asked a group of about 200 homeschool moms to tell me what they felt was their primary responsibility in the home. I wrote down what they said on a whiteboard as women all over the room answered the question:

- Household management
- Child training
- Bill paying
- Homeschooling
- Children's Activities Coordination
- Date Nights (making sure they actually happen)
- Meal Planning

Next, I asked them to tell me what they felt their husband's primary responsibilities were. The moms said:

- Provider/Spiritual Leader
- House maintenance
- Bill paying
- Car maintenance
- Yard work

Parallel lives. You do your thing, he does his. The thing that strikes me most about these two lists is that they are virtually the same everywhere I have ever asked the question. From Chilliwack, BC, to Atlanta, Georgia, this is a very common reality. Our roles—and this is God's design—are different! Homeschooling simply adds a new dimension to our marriages.

I don't know about you, but I'm *glad* that Jay does his thing and I do mine. I have made it my business not to know how to fix the washing machine when it breaks. I depend on my husband to put on his handyman hat and save the day. Conversely, we have an understanding about how the laundry is done. I would rather run the laundry myself for the same reason Jay would rather I did not attempt to change the belt on the washing machine. It's just not an expertise either of us wants to learn. And that's okay.

The issue here is not "his role vs. my role." It's forgetting that even though we fill different roles within the marriage, we need to fill those roles in such a way that our lives are intertwined with each other, instead of parallel.

A Cord of Three Strands

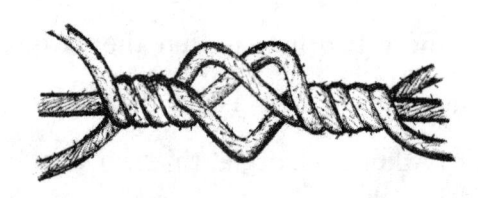

What a difference we see between the two lines that run side-by-side and the cord of three strands that Solomon writes about in Ecclesiastes 4:12, "A cord of three strands is not quickly broken."

The strands of a cord are *intertwined*. That's what makes them hard to break apart. Husbands and wives whose lives are intertwined find that the bond they have is much stronger than when they try to do things on their own.

Of course, the third strand in the cord mentioned in Ecclesiastes is Christ. Without His presence, His purpose, and His peace in our marriage, we left with the world's wisdom. To live lives that are intertwined, we must be intentional about the way we live.

When life seems to spiral out of control in one area or another, I have found it helpful to write down what Jay and I are doing together and what we are doing apart. When I notice that we are not spending time together, or when either of us notices that we've lost the passion we need so much, I can almost guarantee that one of these three things is missing:

- Time alone with God
- Time alone with each other
- Time for physical intimacy

Are you living parallel lives? It's easy to do. One good way to know is to simply ask your husband. You may be surprised at his answer. You may even have to wrestle with these things a little. Being real about my marriage has forced me to look at how I am living out love for my husband.

When I finally found the courage to ask him how he felt our lives were intertwined, I used the illustration of the cord with three strands. Very deliberately, I drew lines that looked like this:

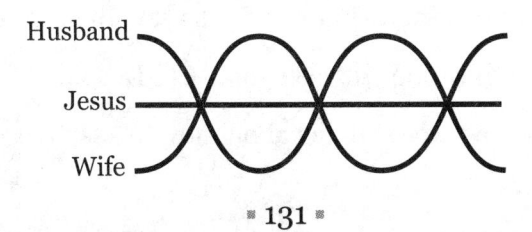

The top line illustrated my husband's life. I drew his responsibilities on the line. On the second line (the straight line) I wrote "Jesus Christ", and on the third (bottom) line, I wrote out my responsibilities.

Do you see the points in which the lines intersect? It's in the middle, where we are spending time reconnecting with each other and with the Lord. It's a simple illustration for a powerful biblical principle, but it really works!

God used this simple illustration to help us tie up some of the loose ends in our marriage. I'll never forget the day that I decided to talk to Jay about this illustration. I pointed out to my dear husband that there were points that intersected and then I asked him what he thought we should be doing together on a regular basis to keep our marriage strong. If you have ever been to one of my workshops, you know what his answer was: he wanted to spend more time with me and saw every space where those lines intersected as an opportunity for physical intimacy. Again, we are so different! I saw those points as times we would spend planning our future, taking walks in the park and dreaming together. (I admit, I also saw them as times for helping me with various household tasks!) Despite these differences, though, we were talking about how to keep our marriage strong. And we were learning new things about each other in the process. It was amazing.

Of course, it's not enough to recognize the negative patterns in our marriages. We need to root them out and intentionally replace them with life-building patterns. We can start simply by making time for each other.

What is the temperature of your marriage? Where do your lives intersect? If it's only at your son's baseball game every Thursday, it's time to re-evaluate your priorities.

Realizing the dangers of parallel living is just one step in a series of steps that shape your marriage. As you purpose to live your lives intertwined as a couple, your marriage will become stronger.

A cord of three strands is not easily broken.

CHAPTER 8
Moment of Truth

YOUR MARRIAGE IS NOT IMMUNE

I've heard it said that a man would swim the ocean
Just to be with the one he loves
How many times has he broken that promise
It can never be done
    ~ "Love Song" by Third Day

The "No Immunity" Clause

Growing up in the 70's and 80's proved to be a very interesting time to learn about marriage. We were still watching re-runs of *Leave it to Beaver* and *The Brady Bunch* but the 60's had left an indelible mark on society as we began to see moral relativism take center stage. Today, secular humanism is everywhere we look. From TV to school text books, marriage is under fire more now than it ever has been. Just pick up a paper or head to the internet for a dose of the day's headlines.

For many years, I believed that because my husband was a pastor, and because we were a "good" Christian homeschool family, we had an edge. But as God began to peel back the layers of my heart, something I had not wanted to see was found staring me right in the eye: I wasn't immune. In fact, I was far from it. I just needed a different perspective.

Just because I could never even *conceive* of looking at another man or betraying the trust of my husband doesn't make me immune. I'm certainly not immune to bad attitudes, prideful conclusions and "other people" pleasing. My strengths can easily become my weaknesses when I fail to yield daily to the truth and gentle voice of the Spirit.

I know you all know this, but I feel compelled to say it again: Homeschoolers are not immune to divorce. Whether you've been through a divorce in your family or you're trying to restore balance to your home and marriage, you must not forget this truth. Why? Because everything in your home depends on nurturing your marriage. Feeling immune to divorce is arrogant—and it sets us up for failure because when we feel like it can never happen, we let our guard down.

And a home left unguarded is a home in trouble.

I'm "All That"

Thinking too highly of ourselves is dangerous. So is thinking too lowly of ourselves, by the way. (That is its own kind of pride.) I like to give pride its own name: I've never been terribly creative, so in lieu of a more creative name, I call him "Pride". Allow me to describe Pride for you:

Pride is a sneak. Have you ever noticed how subtle he is? Pride comes around quietly and even appears righteous on the outside. But the saying "Pride cometh before a fall" isn't just a proverb. It's a fact of life, a law of nature. What goes up, must come down, and Pride will always fall victim to gravity at the end of the day.

In Matthew 23:12, Jesus said, "Whoever exalts himself will be humbled." This is as true in the homeschool movement as it is in the church. Homeschooling doesn't save you, only Jesus can do that.

Pride is a jealous master, too. Pride keeps us from being real with each other.

It's not a popular view among Christians, much less among Christian homeschoolers, but the fact remains—homeschooling won't protect your marriage. The truth is that homeschoolers are not immune to the devastation of divorce. Given the number of homeschooling families these days who are suffering through divorce and remarriage, it's clear we need to be doing a better job of tending to the primary relationship in the home. There is no "Immunity Clause" in homeschooling families.

In fact, the battle for Christian marriage is raging stronger than it ever has. Have you seen its effects on your community? Chances are you have.

Born on a Battlefield

Whether we realize it or not, there's a war going on.

I have come to believe that Christian homeschooling has really gotten the attention of the Enemy of our soul. It's not hard to see why. Parents who recognize the true potential of imparting a Christian worldview to their children have placed themselves directly in the sites of the Enemy.

Why? Because these parents have begun to take back ground that has been a stronghold for the Enemy for decades: the education of God's children.

No wonder Satan is mad. Homeschooling is about much, much more than the ABC's, because education is discipleship. It's a key component to training up our children to live for the Lord in a culture that wars against God.

Busy Homeschool Mom, Are You Ready for Battle?

We have been born onto a spiritual battlefield. The evidence of war is all around us. There is not a week that goes by in our ministry to homeschoolers that we do not hear about a divorce, adultery, pornography struggles, addictions or abuse. As we were traveling the country with our family in the summer of 2009, we heard story after story of broken homes and failed marriages. Homeschool homes. Pastors. Christian parents. "Good" kids.

It's easy to think that homeschooling somehow will make our families immune to the possibility of divorce, but it doesn't. In fact, while doing research for a speaking engagement on marriage and homeschoolers several years ago, I came across the website of an attorney who specialized in helping homeschooling couples get divorced. Business, it appeared, was booming.

Homeschool mom, it's time to get real. Satan's first priority where your marriage is concerned is to drive a wedge between you and your husband. Satan is clever. If he can, he'll use the excuse of something good, like homeschooling, to pull you and your husband in different directions. Homeschooling is a lot of work. It's time consuming. But if you sacrifice your marriage on the altar of homeschooling, the price will not have been worth it.

Homeschooling doesn't make your marriage immune to adultery or abuse. Wearing jumpers doesn't do it. *There is no immunity clause.* When we think "that will never happen to me," and let our guard down, we open the door. We give the Enemy a foothold.

No wonder God admonishes us to be ready for battle! For our own sake, and for the sake of our families, it's time to gird up. It's time to pay attention. Much is at stake.

Reality Hits Home

Part of what makes us who we are is remembering where we've come from. I come from a family that has been absolutely ravaged by divorce. If you are a child of divorce, or if someone close to you has ever been through it, then you know the kind of pain it inflicts. Maybe you're reading this book and you have been through a divorce yourself. It's something we don't like to talk about in homeschooling circles, but we need to.

Since my parents' bitter divorce many years ago, I have become a student of the ripple effect of divorce. In our many years in the pastorate and through personal counseling, we have seen children of divorce suffer terribly, along with their parents.

The culture lies to us about the sanctity of marriage and

the grief of divorce. But I don't think I have ever felt the effects of that lie so strongly as I did during the time we went through a painful divorce with one of my siblings. For two years, we walked beside my sister-in-law as she worked her way through unimaginable grief, loss and betrayal. It tore at the fabric of our extended family. And another pastor's family bit the dust.

We never saw it coming.

But then, we weren't looking all that closely, either.

One Flesh Relationship

The grief was unreal, but God was gracious to us as we helped my sister-in-law put the pieces of her life back together. A little house came up for rent right across the street from us, so she moved back to the Pacific Northwest with her two boys in order to live next to our family.

During this time, I began to see the "one flesh" relationship in an entirely new light. For two years, we spent most of our evenings together. For two years, we cried. Of all the nights we shared together during that time, one stands out to me. On that evening, I noticed a difference in the way she held herself. She seemed to struggle as she walked up the stairs. There was an almost palpable sadness around her.

Jay came into the room and took the boys downstairs to play with their cousins and she and I sat down on the couch—sisters who were grieving the loss in very different ways.

As she laid her head in my lap, she began to weep. If you have ever been around a person who has lost a child, you know the kind of weeping I am referring to. It is too deep for words. It is too raw.

As the tears fell from our eyes, I began to pray for her. This was so unfair! We begged God to intervene, to *do something! Anything* but this! It was worse than a death, it was a betrayal. Death, it seemed, would have been easier. This was cruel. To leave a wife without a husband, and children without their father—when he wasn't dead, but very much alive—seemed more like a made-for-television movie than the true-life story of my pastor brother and his wife.

I remembered another mom telling me one time that her divorce felt worse than death, and I finally understood why. It's not that death itself is not terrible, it's the betrayal of trust and the rejection of a marriage partner that results in a death that is just as real, just as gut-wrenching as a physical death. Divorce is the death of a covenant relationship. The pain it causes is unreal, and in most cases, it's avoidable.

But our new, unavoidable reality was setting in: two young boys would never have their family back again and there wasn't a thing we could do to stop it. I'm not sure what was worse—watching it play out in front of us or feeling helpless to do anything about it.

Time seemed to pass so slowly as we cried together. I can't remember how much time went by that night, but at some point, my sister looked up at me, and said she felt sick. I didn't understand.

"I need to go to the hospital," she stammered. "I feel like my skin is on fire!"

Carefully, I felt her face and looked at her hands. Aside from the wetness of her tears, she felt fine—and then she said the words that are etched into my soul forever:

"I feel like my flesh is being ripped away from me. . . I can't stop it. We're one flesh, my husband and me! I feel like I am going to die from the pain!" Her words trailed off into muffled sobs again. At that moment, I *knew* the power of the one-flesh relationship.

> *Divorce is the death of a covenant relationship.*

It is a bond that God has designed to last a lifetime. When God said, "The two shall become one flesh," He meant it. I wonder how many divorces would never happen if we were to look at marriage with the sense of permanence that God designed it to have? I wonder what the landscape of our Christian churches would look like if we truly preferred one another.

> *I wonder what the landscape of our Christian churches would look like if we truly preferred one another.*

Healing

God is so faithful. After many months of sorrow and little hidden steps of quiet surrender, we began to see healing. It began like a slow thaw after a long winter. And then, a bud appeared on a tree that had but a few branches.

My precious sister-in-law persevered, staying close to her Lord. Learning from Him. Trying to be like Him.

Crying out to Him.

Trusting Him.

One step at a time, God began to make a way through the

wilderness for my sister and her boys.

    He will make a way for you.

    Stay the course.

CHAPTER 9

When It Hurts

HOPE FOR THE BROKENHEARTED

Can I climb up in your lap,
I don't wanna leave—Jesus sing over me

~ "Keep Singing" by MercyMe

Are you weary? Are you broken? Maybe you're reading this, thinking, "I don't have any hope for my marriage." Some of you have experienced first hand the pain of infidelity or abuse, while others of you have held up the brokenhearted before the Lord through your prayers and counseling. God truly is an "ever-present help in trouble."

Over the years, I have discovered that God is faithful. He has been faithful to meet me in times of terrible suffering and pain. Jesus offers us hope.

Because of His great love, we have hope. If your marriage is in trouble, if your heart is wounded, or if you are carrying a friend to the feet of Jesus, be encouraged by the words of Isaiah:

> *"The Spirit of the Sovereign LORD is on me because the LORD has anointed me to preach good news to the poor. He has sent me to bind up the brokenhearted, to proclaim freedom for the captives and release from darkness for the prisoners."*

For some of you, even the prospect of trying to restore a marriage that seems destined to fail is unsavory, even painful. Mix a marriage that's not thriving with the responsibilities of homeschooling and it's easy to forget the big picture. Add a dose of discouragement and suddenly our ears become aware of the Enemy as he whispers, "God doesn't love you. He doesn't care or He would be taking care of you. You could do better than the man you married. Homeschooling isn't worth it. You are a failure. Your marriage doesn't matter. Just give up."

Don't believe it. It's a lie. Your marriage *does* matter and no matter how desperate your situation may look there is always hope in the Lord. Do you remember the story in Matthew 9?

> "While He spoke these things to them, behold, a ruler came and worshiped Him, saying, 'My daughter has just died, but come and lay Your hand on her and she will live' . . . When Jesus came into the ruler's house, and saw the flute

players and the noisy crowd wailing, He said to them, 'Make room, for the girl is not dead, but sleeping.' And they ridiculed Him. But when the crowd was put outside, He went in and took her by the hand, and the girl arose. And the report of this went out into all that land."

~ Matthew. 9:18, 23-26 (NKJV)

Never Too Late

Place yourself in the story and let it sink in. A ruler comes to Jesus distraught, having just seen his daughter die. The girl is dead, beyond hope. Yet Jesus walks into the man's house and disperses the grieving friends and family who have already gathered there, telling them that the girl is simply asleep and not dead.

The Bible tells us that the friends and family ridiculed Jesus. They had watched the girl die. They had closed her eyes shortly after she quit breathing. There was no more sweating, heaving chest gasping for air, sobbing or moaning. Instead there was only silence. The body had already begun to cool off as death settled steadily over the corpse. Rigor mortis may have begun setting in. The crowd turned from grieving to mockery in a moment at Jesus' ridiculous statement. But he removed the friends and family and grasped the girl's hand. Immediately she arose. In Jesus it's NEVER TOO LATE! Even in death when the corpse is cooling and stiffening—it's NEVER TOO LATE!

For all of the well-meaning friends and grieving family there was no foundation of faith. When the little girl died, their world fell apart. Only one man in the crowd had built a firm foundation of God's faithfulness during trials. His faith was simple even in the face of death itself. "My daughter has just died, but come and lay Your hand on her and she will live."

This is why having a foundation for suffering is so important. All that we know to be true in times of rejoicing and all that we teach our children as we mentor and disciple them can easily be lost when trials come.

Some years ago, as Jay and I struggled through a deeply painful situation in our lives, I questioned where God was. I felt so misunderstood, so vulnerable.

> *My suffering revealed a weakness in the way I trusted God.*

And I *was* vulnerable. Vulnerable to attack, to depression, to discontent. My suffering revealed a weakness in the way I trusted God, and I saw that I had a difficult time trusting my heart to anyone, *including* my husband.

After several months of struggling alone, I felt the Lord prodding me to talk to a seasoned homeschool mom who was a veteran of suffering and a dear friend to me. I'm convinced that opening up to her about a weakness in my life was a God-ordained moment because what she said changed my heart.

"Heidi, you must learn never to question in the darkness what God has shown you to be true about Himself in the light."

Those words have come to my mind over and over again in the years that have followed. No matter what the struggle is that you are facing, God remains the same. His love is as constant as the North Star.

Pruned by the Master

I remember attending chapel at Multnomah Bible College back in 1988. In those years, we were privileged to sit under the instruction of Multnomah's founder, Dr. John G. Mitchell, who was in his nineties. We revered this gentle giant. His knowledge of God's word was legendary on campus. He loved the Lord with a passion that I have rarely seen, before or since those days.

One afternoon, Dr. Mitchell walked up to the platform and took a long, deep breath. He opened class with his usual prayer and then he was quiet. You could feel the weight of the words before they came to his lips.

"Do you want to serve the Lord, students?" he asked.

Clapping erupted from the pews. Of course we wanted to serve the Lord! We were at Bible college, for crying out loud. Then, Dr. Mitchell leaned into the pulpit and in a quiet, almost breathless voice he said, "Before God will use you greatly, He will wound you deeply. Are you ready to be pruned by the Master?"

No one clapped. In fact, you could have heard a pin drop in the huge auditorium.

Dr. Mitchell knew the impact of His Words, and so he stepped back from the lectern and stood silently for a few minutes. His Words sank deep into my heart. I began to think back

---

You can't get through suffering in one piece if you are unsure of its refining purpose in your life.

to some very unpleasant thoughts of my childhood and I wondered what more pruning needed to be done.

Of course, there was no way to know what God had in store for us. Dr. Mitchell was just laying the foundation for suffering. He had lived a long time, and we were just babies. He knew something that it would take me several more years to fully understand: You can't get through suffering in one piece if you are unsure of its refining purpose in your life.

C.S. Lewis describes the process of God doing something extraordinary through suffering in his book *Mere Christianity:*

> Imagine yourself as a living house. God comes in to rebuild that house. At first, perhaps, you can understand what He is doing. He is getting the drains right and stopping the leaks in the roof and so on.
> You knew that those jobs needed doing and so you are not surprised. But presently He starts knocking the house about in a way that hurts abominably and does not seem to make sense. What on earth is He up to? The explanation is that he is building quite a different house

> from the one you thought of—throwing out a
> new wing here, putting on an extra floor there,
> running up towers, making courtyards.
> You thought you were going to be made into
> a decent little cottage, but He is building up
> a palace. He intends to come and live in it
> Himself.

Can you even imagine? You and I—dwelling places for the Lord of Hosts! As He builds His home in our hearts, we will feel it. I am convinced that the only difference between those who are mature in their faith and those who are not is the purifying fire of trials. For it is through fire that we learn the truth about our relationships, both with the Lord and with each other.

Learning to Trust

My husband loves the water. Growing up on a lake in northwestern Washington State gave him the opportunity to learn sailing, waterskiing, swimming, and fishing. I grew up in the little town of Boring, Oregon. While we enjoyed visits to the Oregon coast, we generally didn't go out onto the water. In fact, for the most part, we didn't "do" water. Even as an adult, I find that I am hesitant to go out on the water. When the canoe rocks, I get nervous, even though I know how to swim. The family rule about the water and me is: When the mommy is on the boat, don't rock it!

So when I think of the disciples' situation in Matthew 8, my heart goes out to them. Do you remember the storm? This was no April shower, it was a full blown tempest! The disciples were terrified, and the Bible tells us that even those who were veteran fishermen were afraid for their lives. Who could blame them?

As we keep reading, we see that the disciples finally went and awakened Jesus. What? He was sleeping? A storm that terrified even seasoned fishermen raged around them, and Jesus was sleeping through it? I have often wondered why Jesus was sleeping soundly in the midst of such a terrifying ordeal. Surely the boat didn't have cozy cabins and white noise to soothe tired passengers. This was an ancient commercial fishing vessel. Comfort was not a priority, and yet Jesus was sleeping. Can you imagine that kind of peace in the middle of a storm?

What a contrast between Jesus and the men on the boat that day!

Peace instead of fear.

Calm instead of panic.

Jesus found peace, even in the middle of a storm because He knew something the disciples were just learning. Jesus was well aware of the situation. The difference was that *He knew* the One who controlled the seas.

He *is* the Prince of Peace.

He *is* in control.

Nothing New Under the Sun

In Ecclesiastes 1:9, Solomon wrote:

> *What has been will be again,*
> *what has been done will be done again;*
> *there is nothing new under the sun.*

God gave us His Word so we would know the truth; so we would have hope; so we would have perspective. Having eternal perspective is essential to navigating the crazy world we live in. It's easy to be overcome by fear when we forget that what we are facing is nothing new. At least, not to God.

As I write this, the United States is engaged in a war. We are facing one of the worst economic times in our history. The unemployment rate is the highest it's been in over thirty years.

Retirement funds are drying up. Jobs are being cut.

Marriages are failing. Families are hurting.

But God is not asleep. He sees our suffering and He knows our pain. We must put our trust in Him. God's Word says that we have not been given a spirit of fear, but of power and love and a sound mind. Fear is something we all face. But God in His mercy has given us a way out of fear. It is to trust completely in Him.

Praise God for giving us His Word! In the story in Matthew 8, we can easily see our own lives, both private and collective storms raging all around us, and yet Jesus says, "Peace, be still."

Peace. Be still.

Not very easy instructions for a busy homeschool mom like me.

Recently, our friend Gregg Harris spoke at an event we hosted for First Class Homeschool Ministries. As he spoke, Greg began to touch on the importance of leaving things in the hands of the Lord after we are sure that we have done our best. In this way, we can rest and allow God to take care of the details. (Is that as hard for you as it is for me?)

"God is as glad to have you go to bed at night as you are to have your children fall asleep," he said, "because he says the same thing about you that you say about your children! 'Good!

They're asleep! Now I can finally get something done!'"

Amen to that!

Now, peace. Be still. God is on the night watch.

CHAPTER 10

Love for a Lifetime

THE LEGACY OF A REAL LIFE ROMANCE

*When the story of your family is finally written,
what will the record show?*

A Lingering Legacy

I can still remember the thrill of being swung in the arms of my grandpa. Grandpa liked to play "airplane" with us when we were little, and we knew we were in for a treat whenever we would hear the sound of an engine coming from the room where he often sat to prepare for a sermon. Even though he had lived through two world wars and lost both his parents at a young age, Grandpa had a real zeal for life. He and Grandma never missed a basketball game or a cheerleading competition at the small Christian school where they had undertaken the responsibility of paying for our tuition.

When Grandpa picked me up in his arms as a small child

and, later, held me through some of the darkest times in my life, the world seemed safe. I knew that whatever happened, Grandpa would be there. Nothing was too small to share with him. From the scrape on my knee to the final grade on my report card, Grandpa wanted to know the details. Grandpa and Grandma's interest and love motivated me to do well in whatever I undertook in school, because I knew they would be asking me about it in a phone call at the end of the day. They delighted in our successes and chastised us when we blew it. Throughout my childhood, they were constant.

Even though Grandpa and Grandma had hoped to have several children of their own, God was pleased to give them just one child. Their prayers for a bigger family were answered, however, because their one child went on to have seven children—more than enough to keep them busy throughout their ministry and retirement years.

Pastoring is a time-intensive vocation, but we never felt hurried when we were with Grandpa and Grandma. I loved to watch them wink at each other and joke about how they never imagined they could have a granddaughter as smart and as talented as me. (Of course they said this to *all* their grandchildren!)

I remember many times as a newly married woman, when

I didn't know how to handle a problem, Grandpa would stop what he was doing, and come over for a visit. After I got married, my grandparents were still interested in me, except then, their primary interest had shifted to helping Jay and me start off our marriage by encouraging us to build a strong foundation for a love that would last a lifetime. They got it right.

Finishing Well

Of all things I remember about Grandpa, one thing stands out more than any other thing: He knew how to love his wife. Grandpa was a tall, strong man with an infectious laugh and an eye for beauty. I know this because he was always telling us how beautiful Grandma was when he first saw her in the Five and Dime store in Fairbury, Nebraska. To Grandpa, Grandma remained the beautiful store clerk who could beat him at tennis and make him laugh until he cried until the very last day of his life.

Their love affair lasted nearly 75 years.

In May of 2006, we sat around Grandpa one last time. Grandma had been brought over from the assisted living home where they had spent the last five years of their lives. For days, we stood vigil over Grandpa, each grandchild taking a shift throughout the night and day. Someone was with Grandpa and another with Grandma, making sure she was updated on his condition.

We sang over Grandpa, recalling his favorite hymns and reading beloved passages of Scripture to him. Every once in a while, he would open his eyes, and smile at us. Through my tears, I remembered countless hours that he had stood by my bedside as a child covered in chicken pox and later as a new mother, calming my fears and reminding me of all God had in store. It was a time of remembering and we gave thanks for his life as we asked the Lord to have His will.

Death, as it turns out, is a lot like birth. When a child is being born, it is usually not up to the mother, or even to the doctor or midwife to determine the exact moment of birth. Sure, there are signs. In labor, we wait for signs of the transition phase to begin, knowing that it means a more painful, yet hopeful, phase is beginning. The time is drawing close.

Watching my precious grandfather transition from this world to heaven was a lot like waiting for a baby to be born. We saw signs, but he seemed to linger, as if he were waiting for a particular moment. And in his final hours, we learned one last lesson from our grandparents.

We learned the importance of finishing well.

A Final Lesson

As it turned out, Grandpa *was* waiting for a particular moment and that moment came when Grandma visited him for the last time. I'll never forget the love in her eyes—trying to imagine her without him seemed impossible, and yet, she had come to tell him it was okay to go Home. She had come to give him strength and to remind him of what he already knew: God had prepared a place for him.

We lowered the side rails on Grandpa's bed and wheeled Grandma as close as we could to her husband. Then, we stood back with wonder and watched her make one final concession: Grandma was letting her husband know it was okay to go Home.

Her tears dropped quietly onto Grandpa's face. He opened his eyes and puckered his lips. "You're here," he said.

"You didn't think I wouldn't be, did you?" Grandma quipped. And then she spoke to him as if there was no one else in world, let alone in the room.

"Daddy," she said, "I love you. You've been the best husband I could have ever asked for. You have taken good care of me and our family. You are as handsome now as the day I met you and I know I will see you again soon. It's okay to go. It's okay. I'll see you soon—and I know you'll be looking for me. I know it won't be long."

Grandpa, who had not had been able to be hydrated for several days, looked at Grandma. A single tear fell from his eyes.

"I love you too." He said. "See you soon."

Because of my grandmother's great love for her husband, she made the decision to prefer him one last time. Shortly after her visit, Grandpa went home to be with the Lord he loved. Grandma's example set the bar for all of us, even in those final moments.

As I write this, tears fall from my eyes, too, because I remember Grandma's own transition to Heaven just two years later. She was ready to go, and she left this world with Grandpa's picture near her bed and the assurance of salvation in her heart. She knew she would see Grandpa again. Like Grandpa, Grandma, at age 93, had finished well.

I want to be That Girl.

> *Because of my grandmother's great love for her husband, she made the decision to prefer him one last time.*

More Than a Promise

My grandparents made a promise to each other on the day they got married, but I am convinced it was not the words they spoke that kept their marriage strong for over 70 years. In the final analysis, it wasn't the money they had (they lived very frugally) or the possessions they owned that made such an impact on us. It was their love, and their unmatched commitment to the covenant of marriage that has made the deepest impact on my life and subsequently on the lives of their great-grandchildren.

Did they always agree? Of course not. Did they argue? Sure. Did I ever see them fight? Absolutely! Grandma was as stubborn as she was wise and Grandpa knew exactly how to love her around to his way of thinking! In fact, of all the compromises I saw them make for each other over the years, there was one thing I knew they would never compromise: their marriage vows. It was the knowledge that they would work things out that gave me the gift of a secure relationship as a child. It was the best gift they could have given us.

They understood the responsibility and the impact of the promise they made on the day they got married. Grandpa and Grandma knew that the vows they made on their wedding day were much more than a promise. They had made a covenant with the Living God.

Just as surely as my grandparents' marriage affected me, your marriage is affecting your children and the lives of those people around you.

As parents, we set the tone for the generation behind us. By understanding the role that our marriage plays and the importance of holding fast to God's heart and design for our marriages through good times and bad (yes, even through richer and poorer, sickness and health), we discover that God's plan for marriage is bigger than the two people involved.

Marriage is more than an institution. It is a covenant relationship. A promise involving you, your husband and the Living God.

> *Just as surely as my grandparents' marriage affected me, your marriage is affecting your children and the lives of those people around you.*

Finishing Well

In Acts 20:24, Paul told the Ephesian elders that he had a course to finish. Do you know that Paul's course was ordained by God? Many homeschooling moms today don't want to finish their course. They want someone else's course. Can you relate? I know I have felt that way many times in the past twenty years of marriage, kids, and homeschooling.

We need to keep our eyes on the finish line. When we think of our lives as an opportunity to affect the next generation, and when we think of our marriage as more than an arrangement, we can begin to see a greater purpose—a Kingdom purpose. God wants to use our marriages as a witness to the world of His great love. Understanding the fact that we live on a spiritual battlefield becomes a reason to gird up, and resolve to finish well.

Our homes should be places of rest and security. In a hostile and busy world, marriage should be a sanctuary. The culture we live in has abandoned God and His heart for marriage, so it should be no wonder that we have abandoned the sanctity of marriage.

Try to see your marriage as an opportunity to be the wife God has created you to be. When you do, it can change your life. Instead of criticizing your spouse, pray for him. Love him.

Prefer him. Grow old with him. The impact you will have by living out and then leaving behind a legacy of love will reach far into future generations.

Finish well.

Looking Past the Homeschool Years

Busy homeschool mom, you're on an amazing journey.

It's easy to forget how quickly these years go by when we're in the middle of teaching math facts and prepositions. It's understandable to feel overwhelmed by the sheer magnitude of the task that you and your husband have undertaken by your decision to homeschool.

But it's worth it.

Our oldest daughter enrolled in Multnomah University this fall. Like so many mothers before me, I am now learning firsthand how quickly the homeschool years go by. Could this really be the little bundle that scared me so much when I first held her in my arms, overcome with the enormous responsibility of raising her?

She's ready to start her own journey. We're excited to see her take her first steps in obedience to God's call on her life; excited to see her be all that God has created her to be.

As I watched her drive to class for the first time, it occurred to me that this is just the first in a series of "happy" good-byes that we will say to our children in the years to come. And then, our house will return to the way it was when we first stepped over the threshold.

Jay and I recently celebrated our 20th anniversary. Over dinner one night, we noted that we are entering a new season in our lives together. The "growing years" are very likely over in terms of adding children to our own family.

Even this busy homeschool mom, with laundry piles galore, menus to plan and history lessons to teach, can appreciate how quickly time is passing.

Our marriage, indeed our family, is entering a new season. New members will come into the St. John family through marriage from this point on and then the miracle of new life will begin again as we become grandparents some day (I can't believe I just wrote that!).

Sing a Song of Solomon

I challenge you to look beyond the homeschool years and see the big picture. When the homeschool years are over, what will you have? By God's grace, you will be looking into the eyes of the man you married, excited about what God has in store for you as you grow older together.

By God's grace and through his mercy, your husband will look into your eyes and rejoice in the wife of his youth, because he'll see That Girl when he sees you.

By seeing the husband God has given you with fresh eyes, and finding a new perspective and purpose in your marriage, you will begin to discover that even busy homeschool moms need to make time for romance.

So sing a love song, busy homeschool mom. Sing a Song of Solomon. You are That Girl to your husband, to your children, and to the Lord. Create a legacy of love that your children will pass on to their children.

As you give your life over to the One who loves you best, and ask Him to give you a love song that will last a lifetime, get ready to be changed. Get ready to be *That Girl*.

That Girl is . . .

Real. Passionate. Godly. Steadfast. Beautiful. Committed to the pursuit of God's heart for her marriage.

You are *That Girl,* busy homeschool mom! And as you exchange your will for the will of the One who loves you best, I think you'll discover that the best is yet to come.

Let the celebration commence!

ABOUT THE AUTHOR

Heidi St. John is one busy homeschool mom!

She has been happily married to her husband Jay since 1989 and is the mother of six children ranging in age from preschool to college. Heidi is a favorite homeschool convention speaker, member of The Old Schoolhouse speaker's bureau, and author. She has written a number of homeschooling workshops which she presents around the country.

Heidi brings hope and freedom to homeschooling families through laughter and encouragement.

Her passion to help set homeschool moms free from the expectations of others and lean into the Lord will inspire and encourage you—through the homeschool years and beyond.

Heidi and Jay are also the founders of First Class Homeschool Ministries, a parachurch organization dedicated to helping churches start homeschool cooperatives.

For more information about Heidi St. John, or to book a speaking engagement, call

360-326-8826
or go to
www.heidistjohn.com

Homeschool Doesn't Have to Mean Home Alone!

first class homeschool ministries
psalm 1:3

DOES YOUR CHURCH HAVE A MINISTRY TO HOMESCHOOLERS?

First Class Co-ops Are:

- A Complete Christian Homeschool Co-op Program
- An international Network of Co-ops
- An Outreach to your Homeschool Community
- Affordable and Self-Sustaining

Everything you need to start a homeschool co-op.

Request a **FREE** information pack at:
www.firstclasshomeschool.org
360.326.8826

"First Class co-op is the fuel we put in our homeschool gas tanks that keeps us going strong all year long."
~ Niki S.
   First Class Clark County, Vancouver, WA

"Even though we had an established co-op when we joined First Class, it immediately provided the tools and resources to better organize the growing needs of our group. It's also provided a much-needed support network for the leaders. First Class has been an answer to our prayers!"
~ Patty R.
   First Class Folsom, CA

"I would strongly encourage Pastors to consider embracing First Class. Their ability to reach into a segment of the culture in your city will impact your church and ultimately shape and change lives for the Kingdom of God."
~ Rich Wood, Sr. Pastor
   LifePoint Church, Camas WA

"I am grateful for the work you are doing with First Class to keep us from becoming isolated. First Class is an answer to prayer in our community."
~ Claudine A.
   Chilliwack, BC Canada